D1145330

Books are to be returned on ~
the last dat~

04. MAR C

AUTHOR RESS Laurence

TITLE Selling politics

CLASS No. 324·23 BOOK No. 41065

COLLEGE OF FURTHER EDUCATION
SUTTON COLDFIELD
LIBRARY

P52643-B3 (C)

SELLING POLITICS

SELLING POLITICS

Laurence Rees

BBC BOOKS

This book accompanies the BBC television series entitled We Have Ways of Making You Think, broadcast in November 1992.

Published by BBC Books,
a division of BBC Enterprises Limited,
Woodlands, 80 Wood Lane, London W12 0TT

First Published 1992
© Laurence Rees 1992

ISBN 0 563 36388 6

Typeset in 12/14 Horley by Goodfellow & Egan Phototypesetting Ltd, Cambridge
Printed and bound in Great Britain by Redwood Press Ltd, Melksham
Jacket printed by Lawrence Allen Ltd, Weston-super-Mare

Picture Credits (numbers refer to plate pages)
Page 5 (top) Associated Press; 3 (lower) © Phil Huber, Black Star Agency; 1 (lower), 4 (top), 5 (lower), 6 (top), 7 (top) Hulton Picture Company; 8 (top) The Independent Newspaper; 7 (lower), 8 (lower) Network Photographers; 3 (top) © Roger Sandler, Picture Group; 4 (Lower), 6 (lower) Rex Features; 2 "Conceived by Tony Schwartz"; 1 (top) Ullstein Bilderdienst.

Sutton Coldfield,
College of F.E.
LIBRARY.

Acc. No.
4 1 0 6 5

Class. No.
324·23

To Jonathan Gili

Contents

Acknowledgements

I would like to thank all those who worked with me on the television series *We Have Ways of Making You Think* on which *Selling Politics* is based: the Assistant Producers, Edi Smockum and Karen Liebreich; for research in Romania, Simona Toncea, and for research in India, Frenez Khodaiji; all the various camera teams, particularly Jeremy Pollard, John Keeping, Morton Hardacre and Jerry Stein; and the Film Editors, Alan Lygo, Jim Latham and Graham Dean. I am grateful also for the advice of my Executive Producer, Jeremy Bennett, and for the exceptional help and support of our Production Secretary, Harriet Rowe. I thank my wife Helena, Michael Dean, Professor Derek Brewer and Jonathan Gili (to whom this book is dedicated) for their comments on the first draft of the book, and Jackie Walsh for keeping our year-old son Oliver away from the word processor.

Above all, I am grateful to Alan Yentob, Controller of BBC2. It was his idea to make a television series on this theme and his enthusiasm made the project possible.

In the course of research and production of the television series we talked to more than a hundred people in Britain, America, Germany, India, Romania and South America. I hope they will forgive me if I do not list them all here – our thanks are no less sincere for being expressed collectively.

None of the above are, of course, responsible for any errors or omissions in this book. Nor should the views and opinions expressed within it be taken as anyone else's but my own.

Introduction

In the spring of 1991 I was in the plush Manhattan office of one of America's brightest TV political consultants as he confided his propaganda plan for a forthcoming mayoral election in the Mid-West. After a week spent ploughing through research he had at last found a way his candidate could attack the incumbent Mayor.

'We've really got this incumbent with his pants down,' he boasted. 'The research shows that the voters think he's out of touch. And guess what? On the coldest day last year, when your ordinary Joe in the Mid-West couldn't start his car and was knee-deep in snow, guess where the lousy Mayor was – only on vacation in Florida!'

'And?' I prompted, waiting for the punch line.

'And nothing,' he said. 'Don't you get it? We'll make an ad which will intercut the news footage of the bad weather with glamorous shots of Florida palms and beaches. We say: "Whilst you froze, the Mayor was in Miami!"'

'But how could he have known that it was going to snow?' I asked. 'I mean, it wasn't his fault that he was on vacation, was it?'

'Fault?' echoed the consultant. 'Who said anything about fault?'

Here was one of America's most respected political consultants about to make an ad which purported to show that the incumbent Mayor of a Mid-Western town was out of touch because he had happened to be on holiday in Florida when there was a snowstorm at home. The ad (never made for lack of campaign funds) would have exploited the propaganda powers of television perfectly. No analysis, no attack based on political issues; just an impressionistic, emotional and unanswerable picture of a politician who was so out of touch that he was basking in the sun whilst everyone else froze.

This book is about the work of such men (and all the leading consultants are men). It seeks to examine the inter-relationship between television and politics, particularly the way in which television is used as a medium for propaganda and political manipulation. It argues that the consultants have managed to learn certain truths about the medium of television which they exploit ruthlessly, often working the considerable trick of producing propaganda (like the proposed 'snow' ad) which is unfair yet unanswerable.

In America today the influence of the 'political consultant' is pervasive. Twenty years ago there were a hundred of them; now there are ten thousand. Raymond Strother, a veteran Democratic consultant, put it simply: 'In America today without good professional help, if you're running against a person who has professional help, you have virtually no chance of being elected.' Strother's use of the term 'professional help' is typical of the euphemisms that almost all the consultants I talked to used for their work. They are chary of being described bluntly as propagandists, though according to the dictionary definition of the word 'propaganda' ('organized scheme for propagation of a doctrine or practice') that is precisely what they are.

Selling Politics is concerned primarily with the work of the American political consultants, the men who work at the cutting edge of television propaganda. But it does not follow that a study of their work is only of interest to the American reader. For although first developed in the United States, their propaganda techniques have subsequently appeared in other countries, particularly Britain. Both the Conservative and Labour parties have looked to America for inspiration. John Profumo visited the United States to study the American Presidential campaign of 1952, Sir Gordon Reece examined the 'photo-opportunity' in America in the 1970s, and recently the Labour party employed the American consultants

Doak and Schrum. Prior to the 1992 election there was even a secret meeting between Shaun Woodward, the former Conservative Director of Communications, and the notorious American propagandist Roger Ailes, the man behind the infamous furlough ad shown during the 1988 Presidential election (see page 105). Such is the dominance of the American consultant in the field of propaganda that many of them make a good living working in foreign countries. Significantly British propagandists do not work in the United States. The stream of propaganda influence is one way – from the United States to Britain.

This book asserts that it is the medium of television itself which has allowed the American political consultant to flourish. But there are those, notably Professor Kathleen Jamieson, who argue that television is just another delivery system for political messages – indeed, that the medium merits no unique insight. In her monumental work *Packaging the Presidency* she points out that in the nineteenth century handbills were circulated which falsely accused candidates of nefarious crimes. In the same period the 'pseudo-event', so beloved of today's propagandists, was flourishing. She tells how, in the Presidential campaign of 1840, Daniel Webster 'camped with Green Mountain boys in a pine wood before an open fire, ate meals from shingles, paid tribute to log cabins and challenged at fisticuffs anyone who dared call him an aristocrat'.

At one level Professor Jamieson is, of course, right. Trivial, negative and emotional campaigns have often been a feature of American (and not only American) politics. But television is influential in a way that handbills and primitive 'pseudo-events' were not. Television *of itself* has changed politics. This proposition first emerged in Marshall McLuhan's seminal work *Understanding Media*, and more recently Professor Neil Postman of New York University came to the same conclusion in his *Amusing Ourselves to Death*. In essence, what both McLuhan and Postman are saying is that we mustn't look on television simply as another medium through which thoughts, opinions and personalities can be transmitted. Television has changed the very way it has become necessary to communicate, and thus the very way it has become necessary to formulate political discourse.

Take the question of the importance of the physical appearance of politicians. Abraham Lincoln could have walked down the main street of almost any town in America without being recognized. Millions voted for him because of the views he had expressed; his physical appearance was irrelevant. But for today's politician, appearance is highly relevant, for the first impression a person makes on television is a visual one. This causes at least one leading American consultant to maintain that Abraham Lincoln would be unelectable today. Lincoln's strengths – his thoughtfulness, his literacy, his political experience – are simply not of major importance today alongside the propagandist's new requirements for a Presidential candidate: physical attractiveness, wealth (or wealthy friends), charm and 'likeability'. This is a clear case – and this book attempts to show that there are other similar cases – where the medium has *changed* the nature of politics. Politically unregulated television of the sort permitted in America naturally leads one to the conclusion that today's ideal candidate is less like Abraham Lincoln and more like Johnnie Carson. If this is the case, then the assertion that television has changed politics fundamentally is self-evidently true.

That being so, we need also to reformulate our own views and promote further, more politically desirable change. This book recognizes the power of television and is a call for a better understanding of its nature. At no time in the history of political life has such an understanding been more necessary.

Selling Politics argues that the influence of television-inspired criteria of judgement on politics has been underestimated – particularly in America. There are obvious reasons why this has happened, not least that it is in the interests neither of the politician nor of his propagandist to stress the importance of TV in case they should each be thought 'trivial'. Yet time and again we see both politicians and their propagandists operating in ways that demonstrate how they *have* altered their behaviour to conform with the demands of TV. Not all TV consultants are as open as Michael Deaver, President Reagan's closest White House aide, who told me that while working for Reagan he decided to become 'a better producer' than the networks themselves, on the basis that if he achieved this aim then the networks would 'buy my product'.

Television has had an impact on American society that is

impossible to quantify accurately. But we can be sure that television is the medium through which most people primarily form their view of the world. Only personal experience is a greater influence on opinion-forming than television, and even personal experience is increasingly related in TV terms – witness the American pilots interviewed on TV during the Gulf War who could not recount their experience of combat without reference to the Hollywood film *Top Gun*. We should not be surprised that TV and film values have become the standard of judgement, for as the *Washington Post*'s Paul Taylor says: 'Today there are more TVs than toilets in American homes. The typical household keeps a set on for seven hours and two minutes per day. By the time a baby born when the coaxial cable was laid reaches seventy, he or she will have spent more than seven solid years watching television.'[1]

TV consultants themselves are the first to appreciate how television has changed the political landscape. Roger Ailes states that the purpose of his writing is to show 'how television has changed all the rules of communication and why it affects you more than you think'.[2] Ailes is positive about the benefits of the medium. Indeed he writes, 'I often think television has done so much good for people that I hope they have television in heaven.'

Others disagree. Professor Postman told me: 'What I would object to is their trying to claim that this new kind of politics is good for us. It isn't. It degrades us. It keeps people cynical about and indifferent to the voting process.' This book examines Ailes' claim that TV should be a necessary heavenly appliance, along with the allied view that TV consultants have not of themselves harmed political life.

A common objection to detailed study of the work of today's TV consultants is that, in essence, the effectiveness of propaganda is hardly relevant. Critics say that advertising cannot change firmly held views, and that if a political party has an unpopular policy then no amount of presentational glitz can help the candidate. Political commentators in Britain were quick to point to the skilful Hugh Hudson 'Kinnock' party election broadcast in the 1987 British General Election and to say, in effect, 'Great ad – shame they lost'. To which the answer should be: 'Remember that propaganda skills will give you the edge that *can* make a difference.' Professor Popkin puts it well when he states that voters make up their mind on who to vote for based on a combination of 'past experience, daily life, the media and past campaigns'.[3] All of these elements are susceptible to influence from the propagandist. Presentation *can* influence the selection of individual candidates and thus the content of political policy. If the candidate's television presentational techniques are inadequate, this does not simply mean that he loses an opportunity to put his point across effectively; it means he will be judged an incompetent politician. Most voters are so steeped in TV and its values that the ability to come across well on television is one of the basic skills that a politician now needs – perhaps the most fundamental, for without good television presentational techniques (certainly in America) it is next to impossible to get elected.

Another common error is to suppose that the powerful have little need of propaganda techniques, since they merely exercise their power regardless. 'What does it matter that Hitler had Goebbels?' such people say. 'Hitler had the political power to *make* people do what he wanted.' Of course, if a dictator holds a gun to your head and asks you to recite a particular slogan then (if survival is more important than principle) you will be best advised to recite it. But any totalitarian who operates in such a way is making a grave communications mistake, for as soon as the gun is removed you will detest him and disbelieve his slogan. The case of Nicolae Ceausescu, discussed in detail in Chapter 7, demonstrates how the Romanian dictator made just such an error. If, instead of showing mind-numbingly dull TV propaganda, Ceausescu had followed the advice of Goebbels – who in a famous speech talked of the necessity of 'winning the hearts' of the people – and transmitted *entertaining* propaganda, then it is possible that the Romanian dictator might not have fallen. A population entranced by propaganda is a population which would, given the opportunity, actually *vote* the dictator back into office. That is how important propaganda skills are. They are the difference between success and failure; in Ceausescu's case, between life and death.

Several of the chapters in this book start with reference to the work of Dr Josef Goebbels, a dead and personally discredited figure. This may seem incongruous in a book which is primarily about the contemporary democratic use of television as a means of political persuasion and manipulation. But the plain fact is that the more the work of contemporary 'communicators' is examined, the more, in most respects, Goebbels has been there before them. Goebbels was undeniably a nasty piece of work, but he was a genius in his chosen field and one should be prepared to learn from nasty people as well as nice ones. He was a man who anticipated and reflected popular taste, and it was with a growing sense of surprise that I realized, after we had interviewed many of those who knew and worked with Goebbels, that were he alive today he would be influencing people not through news or current affairs programmes, but through game shows, soap operas and comedy.

All achievement is an interaction between ability and opportunity, and it was Goebbels's good fortune to be working at a time when the 'talkies' were beginning. Goebbels subsequently invented many of the rules of visual propaganda – the idea of the 'snow' ad which was to contrasting the icy Mid-West with sunny Miami could have been devised using his guidelines – and the effectiveness of his methods can be seen on our television screens every night.

Notes

1. Taylor, Paul: *See How They Run – Electing the President in an Age of Mediaocracy*

2. Ailes, Roger: *You Are the Message*

3. Popkin, Samuel L.: *The Reasoning Voter*

Chapter One

The Great Truth

In the spring of 1940 Josef Goebbels ordered a special bus to transport the cast of the recently completed film *The Queen's Heart* (a sympathetic portrayal of Mary Queen of Scots) to his country estate in the woods of Lanke, north of Berlin. Amongst the cast was a beautiful dark-haired young actress called Margot Hielscher, whom the Reichsminister had taken a particular fancy to. On her arrival she was entranced by Goebbels. 'He was very charming,' she says. 'I never would have thought that a politician would have such a routine in handling the females.'

After a traditional Rhineland meal of sausages and mash (the Reichsminister apparently mashed the potatoes himself), Goebbels announced that he had prepared a wonderful 'treat' for the cast.

That night they watched one of Goebbels's favourite movies, a film banned to ordinary Germans because of the profound harm he thought it could do. The film was *Gone with the Wind*.

Goebbels adored *Gone with the Wind*: he was almost obsessed with the story of Rhett Butler and Scarlett O'Hara. 'He saw *Gone with the Wind* at least twenty or thirty times,' says Fritz Hippler, one of Goebbels's most trusted film directors, 'and every new crowd of guests was shown this film as an example.'

Goebbels's love of *Gone with the Wind* is the key to understanding the power of his own propaganda methods. He was not only the first man to realize the true persuasive potential of the medium of film, he was the first to develop the 'Great Truth' about the propaganda use of the medium – an insight that can be summarized thus: in order to be effective, film propaganda must first be entertaining. As Fritz Hippler puts it, 'Each film, including the ones demanded by the state, was meant to be entertaining, not boring, because it makes no sense to make propaganda when the one who had to be captured by the propaganda goes to sleep.' It was no use making films which simply trumpeted the glories of Nazism. The people might be made to watch such crude propaganda, but they could never be made to like it.

Goebbels cared deeply about whether the audience enjoyed the films he made, often poring over box office returns to see what the customer reaction was to a particular favourite. Other totalitarian propagandists like Saddam Hussein or President Kim have mostly ignored what their captive audience actually thought of their work. This has been their single biggest communications mistake. A captive audience is not necessarily a receptive one.

It was an insight that seems to have come to Goebbels during a viewing of the earlier film classic *Battleship Potemkin*, Eisenstein's masterpiece. 'This is a marvellous film without equal in the cinema,' he wrote. 'Anyone with no firm political conviction could become a Bolshevik after seeing this film. It shows very clearly that a work of art can be tendentious, and even the worst kind of ideals can be propagated if it is done through the medium of an outstanding work of art.'

The 'Great Truth' recognized by Goebbels, that all film (and by extension television) propaganda must first be entertaining, has been concealed behind the common historical perception of Goebbels as the 'evil genius' responsible for such works of horror as *Der Ewige Jude* (*The Eternal Jew* – the notorious film which showed rats intercut with pictures of Jews). The truth is that Goebbels disliked most of the crude anti-Jewish films. His ambition was to make a film as artistically fine as *Battleship Potemkin* or as emotionally powerful as *Gone with the Wind*. 'Goebbels was movie-crazy,' says Arthur Rabenalt, a successful film director of the period. 'He liked to watch pretty women and so he liked exactly the same thing as the audience wanted.' He was the least didactic of men. Other cinema favourites included Garbo in *Ninotchka*, *Mrs Miniver* and Walt Disney's *Snow White and the Seven Dwarfs*.

Goebbels was master of the paradox that propaganda must first be entertaining, but pure entertainment can also be propaganda. Arthur Rabenalt puts it this way: 'The political intention of the unpolitical film was that each unpolitical film had a political purpose – to get the audience off the streets, away from the worries of the household and the family and to entertain them.'

The Reichsminister knew that by providing films that were purely entertaining he *was* providing propaganda – propaganda which showed how much the Reich cared for its people, how much the Nazis were concerned that the people would find some escape from the rigours of war. The need of the masses for escape became especially marked after the German defeat at Stalingrad. In 1943 Goebbels watched long queues form outside cinemas immediately after a series of heavy air raids, and wrote: 'People crave recreation after the gruelling days and nights of the past week. They want solace for their souls.'

Goebbels believed so profoundly in the influence of entertainment-based films that when all else failed, when there was no other way of countering the enemy, after he had tried propagating fear, enmity and hate, he turned once more to entertainment. In 1943 he released one of the most charming and colourful entertainment films of the period – *The Adventures of Baron Munchausen*. And in early 1945, when he must have known defeat was inevitable, he ordered troops diverted from the front line to act as extras in a historical drama, *Kolberg*. Entertainment was the ultimate propaganda panacea.

Not surprisingly, Goebbels was under pressure from other senior members of the Nazy party to deliver more conventional 'propaganda'. 'They said: "Where is the film about the Labour Service?"' says Rabenalt. '"Where is the film about the Hitler Youth? Where is the film about the German woman? Where are all these films?" And none of them materialized.'

The Reichsminister was so confident in his vision of the purpose of film that he resisted such pressure. Fritz Hippler, who knew him well, believes that Goebbels recognized the power of film in a profound way, that Goebbels knew that 'the articles in the papers or what was said on the radio influenced the brain, the consciousness, the intelligence, the imagination, while the real primary forces of men are moved by the unconscious, that which he doesn't raise into his consciousness, but which drives him on from beyond his consciousness. On these primary sources, the moving picture works in a particularly intensive manner, and this medium he therefore wanted to use in a particularly pointed way.'

Because Goebbels realized that film was working on the 'real primary forces of man' and not on the intellect, he knew that a number of important and far-reaching consequences followed. The first was that a propagandist who strives first to entertain should never try to *tell* anyone anything. Information is rarely entertaining, for it appeals to the intellect. Entertainment, on the other hand, is, because it appeals to the emotions. If a propagandist can find a route through to his audience's emotions, can change how they collectively feel, then he can have a profound influence. Emotions cannot easily be challenged intellectually, so once a 'feeling' is created it is harder to dislodge than an opinion formed by mere reason. This was a profound insight into the propaganda power of film, an insight that was later to be fundamental to the success of the television propagandists who followed Goebbels.

Even when he found it necessary to insert more conventional propaganda content into his entertainment films, he always felt that if the audience registered the propaganda consciously then he had failed. He never wanted viewers to be conscious of watching a work designed to influence them politically. This is one of the main reasons why Goebbels loved film. No other medium before the invention of television could have had such a wide appeal – an appeal based upon an unintellectual approach. Goebbels's diaries are full of despair at the 'intellectual' attempts of directors to influence film propaganda (and bear in mind that Goebbels was himself the most intellectually gifted of the Nazi elite). On 12 January 1940 he writes of Arthur Rabenalt: 'Check the film *White Lilacs*. Unfortunately a failure from Rabenalt. I am a little depressed by the way our directors start with a success and then always go off the rails and become intellectual.' In December 1940 he writes (and one can almost hear the irritation): 'Intellectualism is the worst enemy of propaganda. I am constantly affirming this.'

From the first day Goebbels took office as Reichsminister of Propaganda in 1933, at thirty-five the youngest minister in any government in the world at the time, he made film propaganda his most important priority. In the early years of his control, film-makers often made the misjudgement of Goebbels that much of popular history has made since. They imagined Goebbels to be a charmless, humourless Nazi hard-liner. It is not difficult to see how they might have reasoned: 'He's a Nazi, and Nazis like marching. So we'll give him what he wants – plenty of parades.' They realized their mistake when they saw Goebbels's reaction to early films like *Hitlerjunge Quex*, the story of a heroic boy in the Hitler Youth who, during the film's climax, ascends to a Nazi heaven and finds it peopled by symmetrically marching stormtroopers. The Reichs-minister hated such heavy-handed work. 'If I see a film made with conviction,' said Goebbels, 'then I will reward its maker. What I do not want to see are films that begin and end with National Socialist Parades. Leave them to us, we understand them.'

Goebbels exercised ruthless control over the German film indus-try, especially over the content of the newsreels. Every Sunday evening Fritz Hippler, head of newsreel production, would drive out to Goebbels's house with the rough cut of the proposed films for the following week's cinema newsreel. Then he would take notes of the changes in picture and script demanded by Goebbels. There would be another viewing with Goebbels late on Monday, for him to give his final approval to the film before it was released to the cinemas.

The Reichsminister would also interfere in every detail of the making of German feature films: scriptwriting, directing and casting – particularly casting. At times his conduct mirrored the excesses of the Hollywood 'casting couch' producers. Goebbels was not simply concerned with which actress was best for a particular film; he was also influenced by which actresses would go to bed with him. As the price of being cast he often insisted that the leading lady slept with him. Many did so willingly. Rabenalt recalls asking one leading actress why she had succumbed, and she replied, 'He just interested me. I wanted to know a man of world history. You don't miss out on that kind of thing.' Goebbels slept with hundreds of young starlets, but without any emotional intimacy – he even insisted that they still call him *Herr Reichsminister* during sex.

Hitler shared neither Goebbels's love of actresses nor his love of Hollywood entertainment films. He wanted propaganda that spoke in obvious terms to the masses. In *Mein Kampf* he wrote: 'The receptive powers of the masses are very restricted, and their understanding is feeble. On the other hand, they quickly forget. Such being the case, all effective propaganda must be confined to a few bare essentials and those must be expressed as far as possible in stereotyped formulae.' Hitler never said it was a precondition of effective propaganda that it should first be entertaining. Despite Goebbels's professed hero-worship of Hitler, a disagreement on this point between the Führer and his Reichsminister for Propaganda always seemed possible. Just such a disagreement eventually occurred over propaganda against the Jews, a subject always dear to Hitler's heart.

During 1939 Goebbels told Fritz Hippler that newsreel cameramen in Poland should take film of the Jews of Warsaw. He told Hippler he needed these pictures for the German archive because 'at some foreseeable time' all these Jews were going to be 'transported to the East'. Goebbels wished to have a record of Jewish customs made, just as an anthropologist might make a film of a jungle tribe before their way of life becomes extinct. On 17 October Goebbels records in his diary: 'Hippler back from Poland with a lot of material for the Ghetto film . . . . Never seen anything like it. Scenes so horrific and brutal in their explicitness that one's blood runs cold. One shudders at such barbarism. This Jewry must be eliminated.'

He then realized he could create propaganda from this 'horrific' material. On 28 October he wrote: 'In the evening look at films. Rushes for our Jew-film. Shocking. This film will be our biggest hit.'

Hippler recalls how Goebbels saw the rough cut of the 'Jew-film' (which came to be known as *Der Ewiger Jude – The Eternal Jew*) and said he 'liked it very much'. But shortly afterwards he ordered the film to be recut. Alterations were constantly demanded, each new version becoming more bloody and aggressive.

On 3 November Goebbels had written, 'The Jew-film is very good', but by the 11th he was writing, 'I work on the Jew-film, the script still needs considerable revision. Discussion with Hippler on the film's future form.' On 10 December he wrote, 'The Poland film (i.e. the Jew-film). Turned out quite excellent. A bull's eye! I am very happy with it.' Yet on the 13th he records: 'Work long hours on films and the newsreel. The Poland film too had to be re-edited yet again at the Führer's wish.' So we now suspect that it was Hitler who wanted the changes. It was Hitler who wanted the film to be so horrific. Fritz Hippler says: 'Hitler wanted to bring the "evidence" so to speak with this film that the Jews are a parasitic race within men, who had to be separated from the rest of men.' As a result of Hitler's personal interest in the film, Hippler says, 'Goebbels demanded rat scenes because rats were portrayed as a symbol for Jews.'

More months passed, and still the 'Jew-film' had not been completed to the Führer's satisfaction. The constant cutting and recutting seems to have wearied even Goebbels. On 12 January he wrote: 'I shall have to rework the Jew-film again.' Eventually, in late spring 1940, the film was released. It was a flop. Some scenes depicting the slaughter of animals according to Jewish rites were so disgusting that women fainted. As Hippler now puts it laconically, 'The demand of the audience was not there. While other films were sold out, the demand for this film at the ticket office was lacking.'

There is no direct criticism of Hitler's judgement over the 'Jew-film' in Goebbels's diaries – he was, after all, intending them as a posthumous documentary record of the greatness of the Third Reich, the Führer and his own role in it all. But there is an entry in his diary on 5 July 1941 which illustrates their diverging approach to propaganda. Goebbels wrote: 'A few disagreements over the newsreel. The Führer wants more polemical material in the script. I would rather have the pictures speak for themselves and confine the script to explaining what the audience would not otherwise understand. I consider this to be more effective, because then the viewer does not see the art in it.'

So the reputation Goebbels received after his death as the master of crude, vicious and evil propaganda is misplaced. On the contrary, he tried his best to provide the German people with entertaining propaganda. In November 1942 he wrote, 'It really seems to me that we should be producing more films, but above all, lighter and more entertaining films which the people are continually requesting.'

Goebbels must have been overburdened with regrets as the war neared its end: regret that the Reich was over, regret that he felt compelled to take his own life, regret that he had never succeeded in making a film as good as *Battleship Potemkin* or *Gone with the Wind*. But had he known the future he would have had yet one more regret: that he did not live to master the medium that would have been even more to his taste than film, a medium born for the intellectual who realizes that the key to its propaganda mastery is its lack of intellectuality. Even more than with film, Goebbels would have exercised mastery over the propaganda power of television. The irony is that many of the propaganda truths he discovered about film were laboriously reinvented by television propagandists a generation later. That rebirth occurred appropriately enough in the New World – specifically in Manhattan in the early sixties.

A new world of propaganda

In 1980 I was lucky enough to meet the grand-daddy of American commercial TV, the man whom David Halberstam in *The Powers That Be* described as 'the greatest huckster of them all', the founder and chairman of the board of CBS, William S. Paley. In an interview for the BBC, conducted in his penthouse suite at CBS headquarters on West 56th Street in Manhattan, he sat surrounded by items from his exquisite art collection and expressed polite incomprehension at the notion that there was any criterion for providing an honourable TV service other than simple viewer demand. 'We give them what they want,' he told us. 'It's called democracy.' The idea of 'public service' broadcasting, of providing programmes which are uneconomic to make but which the broadcasters on behalf of society feel ought to be made, was wholly alien to him. 'The ordinary guy gets home at night,' he said. 'He sits down in front of the TV, he's had a hard day at work. He opens a can of beer. He doesn't want to see opera, he wants to see *I Love Lucy*.'

It was under the pressure of the unbridled commercialism created by men like Paley that American politicians lurched into television. The medium as it developed in America was wholly commercial, wholly audience-driven. And what do the audience crave? They crave just what Mr Paley so successfully and profitably gave them for all those years – they crave entertainment. From the first, the American politician would have to compete on TV not just with entertainment-based programmes, but with entertainment-based adverts. It was inevitable that this simple fact would mean politics would have to change – with some politicians facing up to the new reality more quickly than others.

It was poor Adlai Stevenson whom history cast as the dinosaur of the television age, the man who tried to press on as if nothing had happened. Stevenson, a literate and highly intelligent man, challenged Dwight D. Eisenhower for the Presidency of the United States in 1952 and 1956, and lost both times. He belonged squarely to the age of the 'stump' speaker, an age that it's hard for those of us born into the television age to imagine. Professor Postman in *Amusing Ourselves to Death* paints a romantic picture: '. . . the tradition of the "stump" speaker was widely practised, especially in the Western States. By the stump of the felled tree or some equivalent open space, a speaker would gather an audience, and, as the saying had it, "take the stump for two or three hours".' Such politics are still practised in the few remaining countries that television has not yet quite colonized. In India, for example, politicians who visit villages are still sometimes expected to speak for several hours as a test of their erudition. They are still expected to convey a message of information rather than entertainment.

Stevenson clearly reasoned that the simple purpose of television was to convey his 'stump' speech. One sympathizes with him. On first acquaintance it must have been hard for an intellectual to understand that television was not merely a conveyor of political messages but a changer of messages. Stevenson thought of himself as a 'writer'. He would be seen constantly altering his speech right up to the moment of the 'live' television broadcast. For him the most important aspect of his television performance was the fluency of his words. So spare a thought for his poor producer, who realized that a single, endless shot of Stevenson – not a particularly attractive man – reading his speech to camera was going to have to compete for viewer attention with professional products like *I Love Lucy* and the ads for Ford automobiles.

Stevenson's TV campaign was doomed to failure, especially since it was pitted against that of General Eisenhower, whose team of TV experts coached him in a format entitled *Eisenhower Answers the Nation* in which the candidate gave short, snappy answers to short, snappy questions posed by various stooges. 'That an old soldier should come to this,' Eisenhower is reputed to have murmured in the studio during the recording. But this particular old soldier knew enough to realize that he had to learn new tricks if he wanted to become President. In particular, he knew that he must listen to and trust his television consultant.

Stevenson's conception of the role of his TV consultant is recorded by Professor Jamieson in *Packaging the Presidency*: 'One morning at 1 a.m. during the Democratic convention in 1956, Stevenson summoned William Watson, who had produced his live political broadcasts in the primaries. "I'm having terrible trouble with my television set," said Stevenson, "the reception is very bad, and I wonder if you could drop down and fix it?"'

Why didn't men like Stevenson recognize at once that television was a medium of political persuasion like no other? Perhaps it was because they feared the truth – that television would change political life. In one telling TV advert in 1956 Stevenson announced that TV 'isn't going to stop me campaigning, I'm still going to go out and meet people'. But TV was to change almost everything, campaigning included.

One of the first Presidential candidates to spot the growing influence of television was John F. Kennedy in 1960. Theodore Sorenson, Kennedy's speechwriter, recalls that on a trip through West Virginia Kennedy spotted the 'tiny ramshackle shacks with no plumbing and no newspapers or magazines, but with large television aerials. He had seen surveys showing twice as many Americans citing television as their primary source of campaign information as those citing press and periodicals.'

Just what were the propaganda rules of this powerful new medium? In the fifties and early sixties politicians and their advisers stumbled around searching for the answer. But Dr Goebbels could have told politicians the truth at once. After all, he had already discovered it. Since television, like film, is a medium of entertainment, it follows that politicians must produce entertaining propaganda. One man, more than any other, began to exploit this truth in work which followed, however unconsciously, in the footsteps of Goebbels. His name is Tony Schwartz.

The 'Great Truth' – rediscovered

Tony Schwartz has lived and worked in the same brownstone
building on West 56th Street in Manhattan for thirty years. He
began his advertising career by making radio commercials, and came
to believe that the ideal commercial should tell the viewer or listener
nothing new. Radio and television were mediums of emotion and
feeling. (Bear in mind that an entertainer does not try to inform his
audience, but to touch their emotions and influence their feelings.)

Schwartz maintains that television propaganda (or 'persuasion' as
most Democratic political consultants politely term it) should key
into information already in the viewer's mind. 'With electronic
media we're dealing with *evoked* recall,' Schwartz told me. 'You have
to relate what *you* want to tell me to *my* interest.' Schwartz's key
insight was that television propaganda had to be a partnership
between the propagandist and his audience. This partnership
enables the TV propagandist to cut through the 'clutter' of ordinary
advertising. 'The answer to clutter,' says Schwartz, 'is to talk to
people's interest. They will hear you if you're talking about
something they're concerned with.' So successful television propaganda demands the reverse of the traditional technique of the
'stump' speaker. Instead of the politician speaking on the issues *he*
feels should be of concern to the voters, in today's television age the
politician should research the voters (something Schwartz calls
'pre-search') to discover *their* issues of concern. Then the politician
should address only these specific issues. In a profound way this
renders redundant the traditional concept of politicians as people
who are in the business of trying to persuade voters to convert to
their own point of view. What Schwartz discovered was that
television was peculiarly bad at persuasion, but peculiarly good at
reinforcing previously held views. A politician in a television-led
culture, therefore, should be not a leader but a follower of public
opinion.

Schwartz denies that this is a form of cynical manipulation. 'I use
another word,' he said. 'I'm not manipulating people, they're
involved in what I would call "partipulation". That is they have to

participate in their manipulation. If they don't participate in it, if they want to turn it off or turn to something else, then they can. But if they are bringing things to it then they are participating in their own manipulation.'

The advert that most perfectly demonstrates Schwartz's theory of propaganda (and one that Goebbels himself would have been proud of) was transmitted during a break in CBS's *Monday Night at the Movies* on 7 September 1964. It was an ad paid for by the Democratic supporters of President Lyndon Johnson, and it was so powerful, had such a cataclysmic effect, that it was never shown again during the Presidential campaign. It has become famous under the name *The Little Girl and the Daisy*. In essence the ad is simple: a little girl is picking the petals off a daisy and counting 'One, two, three . . .' As she reaches the number ten the picture freezes and then zooms in to her eye as we hear a missile countdown: 'Ten, nine, eight . . .' down to one. There follows a picture of a nuclear explosion over which we hear President Johnson's voice intone: 'This then is the choice, whether to love each other or to go into the dark. We must love each other or die.'

The Little Girl and the Daisy is a seminal work in the history of television propaganda. There are several lessons to be learnt from its success. First, the advert, true to Schwartz's theory, tells the viewer nothing new. In fact it's hard to work out quite what it tells the viewer in any intellectual sense. A little girl is pulling the petals off a daisy and then suddenly there is a nuclear explosion – what policy is this addressing? What information is it passing on?

Second, the advert fulfils the most important criterion of Schwartz's theory of 'partipulation' and locks into an issue that the voter is concerned with: the safety of the human race, individually personified by a pretty little girl playing in a field. Who would wish to disturb such a child? Implicit answer: Johnson's opponent in the Presidential election, the Republican candidate Barry Goldwater, who was alleged to have made intemperate statements about the possibility of fighting a limited nuclear war. 'Aha!' the viewer is supposed to feel, and thus *contribute* to the advert, 'this is my greatest fear realized. Barry Goldwater might start a nuclear war.' But the cleverness of Schwartz's work is that nowhere is the real message of the ad actually stated in propositional terms: don't vote for Goldwater – he'll cause a nuclear war. The viewer makes an emotional judgement about what he is seeing: he *feels* that a nuclear war is possible if he votes for Goldwater. And feelings and impressions are almost impossible to dislodge. How can Goldwater refute the ad? No formal charges are laid against him, yet a series of devastating but unanswerable impressions are left in the voter's mind.

Third, the advert is presented as a piece of drama. Here is a pretty little girl in a field who is blown up by a nuclear explosion caused by a trigger-happy President. It's a terrible fairy story in which Goldwater is the hidden figure of evil, a kind of Republican wicked witch. Only this is a futuristic drama with a difference – it is interactive. The voter can stop the fairy story becoming reality by withholding his vote from Goldwater.

Imagine this kind of propaganda conveyed by the written word – for example, an article in campaign literature about a little girl in a field who is plucking the petals off a daisy and is subsequently blown up by a nuclear explosion implicitly caused by Barry Goldwater. It simply isn't credible. But television or film are best suited to this kind of emotional, informationless propaganda, because these are media of entertainment and the key to successful entertainment is a dramatic appeal to feelings rather than to the intellect. Whilst the written word can, of course, be a vehicle for entertainment, words are always more susceptible to challenge and question than images.

Schwartz is proud of his work. He thinks of himself as an 'artist' and a 'designer with sound', a pioneer in a 'post-literate society'. The voters in this society are not informed by the work of people like Tony Schwartz, but he does not think this is a problem. The idea of voters listening to the policies of individual politicians and then coming to a rational decision based on their own interests is alien to Schwartz. He believes that voters now make decisions based on feelings rather than intellect. 'You see, people have no experience with the answers to their problems,' he told me. 'If you had ten politicians in here telling you what to do with the economy, you couldn't know who was right. But if you had ten people here telling you how they feel the economy is affecting people, and if they were all qualified for the office, you could say, "You know, he feels exactly the way I do about this. He'll do the right thing." It's based on your feelings towards him from what he evokes within you.'

Towards a new definition of Politics

The work of men like Tony Schwartz in the sixties established a new
definition of politics. As Professor Postman says, 'One doesn't have
to be an academic to have thought of politics as posing for people
alternative choices in the way they're going to live. And this implies
people having information, having some level of awareness of the
issues so that they would know what choices they have.' Television
and the work of the new political consultants has changed all that.

Just how much it has changed can be gathered from a tale told by
Roger Ailes, President Bush's 1988 media adviser and the current
guru of Republican political consultants. In his book *You Are the
Message* Ailes discloses the method he devised to assess the talent of
TV presenters who fronted local chat shows. He would travel to the
various cities, check into a motel room and watch the presenter's
performance. Nothing wrong with that, you might say. But the
revealing fact is that Ailes would watch the presenter in action *with
the sound turned down*. Ailes writes: 'There may be some ex-
television hosts somewhere in America who are gagging while
reading this because they now know that they lost their jobs because
some guy was sitting in a hotel room watching the television set with
the sound turned off. However, this is a technique that I still use
today with clients in our training course.' This is an extraordinarily
significant admission by the master of today's American TV
propaganda. Here is a man who believes so strongly that TV is an
emotional medium that he forms a value judgement about a TV
presenter's (or politician's) ability without having to listen to what
the man or woman is actually saying. Ailes seems to suggest that the
viewer or voter makes a judgement based entirely on visual clues and
doesn't absorb the content of the message at all.

Ailes states that whenever he is unsure about his reaction to a
particular person he always asks, 'What am I *feeling?*' Emotional
judgement is raised above intellectual assessment. In fact it is not
taking the logic of Mr Ailes's technique too far to suggest that
intellectual judgements of themselves are in some way suspect.
Suppose intellectually you like what a candidate is saying, but

emotionally, and for some inexplicable reason, you feel uneasy about him – on this logic that's a good enough reason not to vote for him. Such a rejection need never be rationally explained.

That such views can actually be treated seriously, let alone publicly voiced by the leading Republican political consultant, shows just how far television has pushed the boundaries of politics towards emotional criteria of judgement. Pause a second, and think how it would be if your own career was conducted along these lines. Your boss could call you in and say: 'I know you've worked hard and you do your job well, but I just feel that I don't like you and I feel you ought to go. So I'm sacking you.'

It follows that the axiom of today's consultants is: 'Forget intellectual content, think of ways of affecting the voter's emotions.' (As Goebbels knew, intellectualism is the worst enemy of propaganda.) So the TV propagandist concentrates on ways of reaching the voter on an emotional level. Which is where the work of a consultant operating out of a converted mill house near Baltimore in Maryland is so significant; for Robert Goodman managed to get a man elected to the Senate on the basis of a song.

The Irving Berlin of politics

Goodman, a veteran Republican consultant whose client list has included such luminaries as George Bush and Spiro Agnew, personifies Goebbels's 'Great Truth'. Goodman's over-riding original ambition was not to be a politician, not to be in government, not to ally himself with any great issue. He wanted to work in the entertainment business. 'I thought I was going to be the next Irving Berlin of this country,' he told me. Goodman's dream was to be a songwriter, and yet he has made a good living as a political consultant. He sees no contradiction in this. 'Music is an emotional element,' he says, 'and we believe, and I think most of our competitors believe, that voting is an emotional act.'

Goodman has always thought of political campaigns as dramas. 'I saw that they were no different from a play,' he says, 'except that these were real actors and actresses on the stage, and I tried to create emotion about my candidates by putting them in environments and writing rousing music to support them so that there would be hope out there.' Through a toothy smile Goodman confesses that, 'Love and hope is what I was selling.' So a political campaign on television is not about defence policy or economic plans or the reorganization of the National Debt; it is, in Goodman's words, 'a classic drama of the man in the white hat and the man in the black hat'. Words are essentially superfluous since in a political campaign, just as in a movie, at a critical moment it is not words but the 'music' which 'swells up'.

Goodman's campaign for a rich Wyoming man named Malcolm Wallop, who ran for a Senate seat in 1976, perfectly illustrates the truth that effective television propaganda should be entertainment-based. Wallop was running against an incumbent senator named Gale McGee. In common with every other modern political consultant, Goodman's first act was to consult the electorate: he polled the voters of Wyoming to establish the issues on which McGee was vulnerable. (It is never done for a consultant to approach a campaign with firm preconceived ideas on policy. Men like Tony Schwartz have proved that TV propaganda must be 'plugged into' the voter's own feelings, not geared to the individual politician's particular beliefs.)

Goodman examined the results and discovered that he and his candidate had a problem. The polls showed that Gale McGee was 'correct on every issue'. The incumbent Democratic senator had no policy weak spot; the voters were very happy with him. But this depressing news only represented a greater challenge to Robert Goodman. He told me that he then sat in a dark room and 'dreamed of Wyoming'. His intuition told him that he should try and connect his candidate to the notion of 'state pride'. 'If you can connect people with pride in a state,' he says, 'you're doing something wonderful because you're taking your candidate and you're saying, "Ah! This is the symbol of Oklahoma or Texas or whatever state."'

Goodman sat in his dark room and dreamed of Wyoming, and as he dreamed he dreamed of – the horse. 'Horses are symbols,' says Goodman, 'they're not just animals. It's not like an automobile. It's not just a conveyance. It's a whole way of life and speaks of independence and self-reliance.' The answer was clear – put the candidate on a horse. But this was only part of the solution. After all, any political consultant might have thought of putting his candidate on a horse. Robert Goodman put Malcolm Wallop on a horse and wrote a song about it.

The advert which Robert Goodman created for Malcolm Wallop is extraordinary. It opens on pictures of cowboys riding at round-up time, and then cuts to a shot of Malcolm Wallop wearing a cowboy hat and riding a horse. He is surrounded by his supporters (who are also, of course, on horses). Goodman had developed the idea of a 'Wallop Senate Ride': his candidate was going 'to ride the state'. As it turned out Wallop only rode his horse about fifteen miles, but then a television camera hardly needs to see a rider for more than a few seconds to make its point. Goodman confesses that his candidate needed 'something outrageous to win this thing', because 'we weren't going to win this thing on the merits of the issues'.

In his dark room Goodman eventually came up with the lyrics for the campaign song to capture the 'feel' of Wyoming:

Come join the Wallop Senate ride,
The Wallop Senate ride,
It's alert and it's alive and it's Wyoming to the spur,
The Wallop Senate ride.

Goodman freely admits that he had trouble selling Wallop's campaign managers the line 'Wyoming to the spur', but he 'really put [his] foot down' and said, 'Now listen, I do the music – let me alone.' The advert neatly sidestepped the problem that Wallop's opponent was 'correct on every issue' by not mentioning any issues at all. Wallop won the campaign, and (at the time of writing) is still in the US Senate.

The Wallop Senate Ride repays as much study as *The Little Girl and the Daisy*, and is probably even more revealing about the truths of TV propaganda. What, for instance, does the voter actually learn about Malcolm Wallop's fitness for high political office from Goodman's advert? That he can ride a horse, true. That he is riding the state, possibly. That Wallop is a cowboy, perhaps. But here the voter is misled. Wallop is not a cowboy. As Goodman admits, 'there was a little stretch there'. Wallop is actually a rich man, educated at Yale University in the East, and his nearest connection with the authentic Western image of the horse was that he bred polo ponies. He is descended from an English aristocrat. This is the background not of a real cowboy but of an ersatz John Wayne. Goodman admits: 'It was a kind of weakness out there that he [Wallop] wasn't exactly born in the saddle.'

So there we have it. A man who is not a cowboy is shown as a cowboy and defeats an incumbent senator who, according to the polls, was 'correct on every issue'. How can this have happened? Only because of television and because of the talent of Robert Goodman. His sixty-second ad is an extremely effective piece of *entertainment*. Goodman manages to make the voter believe that a vote against Wallop was a vote against the values of the West; a vote, indeed, against that ultimate symbol of American freedom – the horse.

Pick a symbol

Symbols are important in television propaganda – much more important than ideas. For Schwartz a little girl picking a daisy represents humanity, represents everyone's family; for Goodman the horse represents the values of the West. Other symbols commonly found in American ads are the Stars and Stripes, the Statue of Liberty, Air Force One, the Presidential seal, the White House, the cowboy, the family and (most important of all as a symbol of the future) children.

The use of symbolism is, of course, the very stuff of dramatic entertainment. A costume designer does more than simply dress the characters in a play. He or she is employed to convey symbolism through appearance. The crown that King Lear wears, the dress of Ophelia, the armour of Macbeth – all are intended to express symbolic meaning. Professor Derek Brewer in his *Symbolic Stories* convincingly argues that even the most primitive stories can have symbolic effect. He quotes Boccaccio: 'There was never a maundering old woman, sitting with others late of a winter's night at the home fireside, making up tales of Hell, the fates, ghosts and the like – much of it pure invention – that she did not feel beneath the surface of her tale, as far as her limited mind allowed, at least some meaning . . .'[1]

If Boccaccio were alive today he could have written just such a comment on current political propaganda. For TV is the perfect medium for both entertainment drama and visual symbolism. 'Beneath the surface' of political ads there is always 'some meaning'. Reagan wants to portray an anti-east coast message – fine, put him on a horse and make him wear a cowboy hat. Carter wants to show he's anti-lawyer – easy, dress him in a gingham shirt and have him walk through his peanut fields at sunset. As one TV consultant put it cynically during Michael Dukakis's Presidential campaign: 'If your candidate is weak on defence, don't change his policy, just hold a photo-opportunity and put him in a tank.'

Since symbols carry no promise, represent no assertion, they are both difficult to refute and easy to mislead with. In the *Wallop Senate Ride* commercial Goodman was at pains not to dress his candidate like an ordinary cowhand but, in his words, to 'dress Wallop *up*. He has a tie on. He isn't ready to take on the bad guys, he's ready to lead'. The viewer is therefore supposed to take in symbolic visual clues, often placed specifically by the propagandist in order to mislead. Goodman admits that, 'If I had a cowboy running I don't know if I'd "over-cowboy" him. I'd try to show the other sides that could relate to other people so that he wouldn't have just a linear image.' This is a revealing comment. It shows just how the clever television propagandist uses symbols, not arguments.

Suppose a cowboy was standing for the Senate. The propagandist would realize that the perception of him would be that he *was* a cowboy – therefore time spent expanding public consciousness on that score would be wasted. But this cowboy candidate might be vulnerable to attack for not understanding *urban* problems. Solution: place him in visual situations where he is interacting with voters such as factory workers who will symbolize urban values. An advert showing the cowboy candidate in such a situation is not open to challenge. But if a manifesto was written outlining in black and white the cowboy candidate's qualifications to deal with such urban problems then he would most definitely be open to attack. Once again, the propagandist makes use of the fact that you can debate a proposition, but you can't sensibly debate an impression.

Leaving aside the fact that symbols can easily mislead, there is another problem with their use. 'I call it the great symbol drain,' says Professor Postman, 'because you can, by frequent and irreverent use of important national symbols, draw all meaning from those symbols.' He quotes the example of a product commercial for Hebrew National Frankfurters in which Uncle Sam is shown pointing to heaven, explaining that Hebrew National Frankfurters go beyond government health requirements and answer to a higher authority. 'So now God is invoked,' says Postman, 'in order to sell frankfurters.' Postman imagines the day in the not too distant future when a wine company 'will use Jesus and show this man in the desert saying that "When I turned water into wine at Cana" (and then he will hold the bottle), "this is what I had in mind."' Thus symbols are torn from their context in order to generate a certain kind of feeling in the voter.

Entertainment criteria of judgement

Television propaganda in America must work first as entertainment because it must survive on its merits in a medium that is fiercely entertainment-driven. In America there is no method available to *make* people watch (and even if it existed it would fail, as Goebbels knew). The political advert must compete successfully against *Dallas* and *Hill Street Blues*, or *Cheers* and *I Love Lucy*. As Professor Postman wrote in *Amusing Ourselves to Death*:

> The single most important fact about television is that people
> watch it, which is why it is called 'television'. And what they
> watch, and like to watch, are moving pictures – millions of them,
> of short duration and of dynamic variety. It is the nature of the
> medium that it must suppress the content of ideas in order to
> accommodate the requirements of visual interest; that is to say, to
> accommodate the values of show business.

As Marshall McLuhan realized thirty years ago, 'The culturally disadvantaged child is the TV child. For TV has provided a new environment of low visual orientation and high involvement that makes accommodation of our older educational establishment quite difficult.'[2] In other words, don't just censure the propagandist – blame the medium which in unregulated form makes it unrealistic to expect a generation raised on television to be able to listen to a traditional 'stump' speech which demands an attention span of over an hour.

Any political propaganda which transmits over the medium of television is immediately judged by the entertainment criteria of the programme content around it. The political advert has to compete with product adverts, images often designed to tell a story-led narrative and to entertain the viewer *before* they try and sell. One can hardly blame the propagandist if he then feels he must create works of entertainment to try to influence the voter. He can do little else if he wants his candidate to be elected. The medium forces entertainment values upon him.

Today's political propagandist must seek to grab his audience swiftly – Roger Ailes believes that we make up our minds about a candidate within three seconds of seeing him. The propagandist must deal with the fact that the use of remote control 'zappers' is growing. In America in 1985 only 29 per cent of households used them; now the figure is 72 per cent. Increasingly viewers switch swiftly from one channel to another in a phenomenon known as 'grazing'. In America the pressure is continually growing not just to entertain, but to entertain swiftly, and with the growth of satellite and cable channels in Europe, it is a pressure that is likely to be felt on this side of the Atlantic as well.

It follows that since TV consultants must at heart remember they are primarily producers of entertainment, then entertainment-based criteria must be used to judge their work. Joe Slade-White, one of the brightest and most imaginative of America's TV consultants, describes how the selection of a consultant has become 'a year-long process, where we go and audition for the candidates and their families and their advisers and their friends and the house dog is brought in and we see if it wags its tail and we go out and literally audition as if we're actors and actresses'.

The most important factor in the selection of a consultant is how entertaining their show-reel of past work is. Joe Slade-White recalls the revealing technique used to select potential consultants by a campaign manager in a contest for the governorship of Illinois. 'His process for narrowing down the field,' Slade-White told me, 'would be to take the demo tapes home with him. On Sunday he would read the Sunday paper and pop tapes into the VCR in the television, and he said if any of the tapes made him look up and watch the screen and turn away from the newspaper, then he would separate those and put them in a special pile.'

This is a selection method of understandable logic. One can imagine the campaign manager thinking himself pretty clever for devising it. 'After all,' he would have said to himself, 'these adverts have to compete on television amongst all the clutter of other TV programmes, and it is established that most people only half-watch television, so the most important quality these adverts must possess is the ability to make me look up from my paper.' The logical conclusion of this is clear: the campaign manager should not have been judging the tapes himself – he was far too intelligent and politically informed to come to a decision as to their worth. Ought he not to have shown them to a more average voter? This is precisely what happened. 'One of the reasons I was hired,' says Joe Slade-White, 'was that the campaign manager had an eight-year-old son and his eight-year-old son would bring his friends over to watch my videotape.' The campaign manager thought if 'an eight-year-old wanted to show the tape to his friends . . . this would be a good way to run a campaign'. Slade-White admits he got the job of making the ads for an $8 million campaign 'on the basis of a critique by an eight-year-old', but says: 'I liked that. I thought that was absurd enough to appeal.'

P.G. Wodehouse once wrote a short story in which a theatrical manager is depicted as asking his ten-year-old nephew to make all creative judgements, since the average mental age of the Broadway theatregoer was thought to be ten. This appears to be the same logic as that by which today's consultants are hired. The only difference is that Wodehouse was writing fiction.

Joe Slade-White is a disciple of Tony Schwartz. He sees nothing wrong in an eight-year-old judging his work because it is designed to appeal to the emotions of the voters, not to their intellect. An eight-year-old could never be expected to make a rational assessment of a candidate's economic plans. But he can make an emotional assessment of a candidate's television performance, because he has had nearly six years' experience of judging television, of turning off a programme he does not like, and of switching between the channels looking for a more entertaining diversion. An American eight-year-old has probably spent more of his waking hours watching television than doing anything else. He is plainly equipped to make a judgement of a television commercial using emotional criteria. 'We all use emotion,' says Joe Slade-White. 'In our daily lives – when you asked your wife to marry you it was emotional. Some of the most important decisions that we make in our lives are done on the basis of emotion, and they're done intuitively and impulsively.'

Think how far we have come. Otherwise sensible, creative men like Joe Slade-White believe that politics is a matter of the emotions and that an eight-year-old is as much entitled to a judgement on political matters as an eighteen-year-old. But economics is not dealt with by the emotions, the National Debt is not helped by a politician's 'feelings'; whether to cut defence spending is not an emotional decision on a par with the choice of one's partner. What would Lincoln have made of all this? His Gettysburg address is hardly within the intellectual grasp of an eight-year-old. 'Fourscore years and what?' the eight-year-old would say. 'Why can't he just say a long time ago, or eighty years? What is all this flowery stuff? I can't make sense of it.' But an eight-year-old *can* understand the speeches of George Bush or Ronald Reagan. It is, of course, television that is responsible for this change. On the small screen, politicians, adverts and soap operas are part of a clutter which is watched by *everyone*, including eight-year-olds. The age when politics was merely the concern of rational adults is past.

The entertainer as President

It may be thought trite to observe that the logical conclusion of all this is that an entertainer would one day be elected President of America – Ronald Reagan. But the more the man and his Presidency are studied, the more perfectly does the Reagan phenomenon fit into the pattern of the expected consequences of entertainment-based propaganda.

Ronald Reagan had one thing in common with Josef Goebbels. They both loved to watch Hollywood movies. According to Lou Cannon of the *Washington Post*, an acknowledged Reagan expert, 'Reagan spent more time at the movies during his Presidency than anything else.'[3] Reagan seems to have absorbed much of his moral value system from Hollywood movies. Michael Deaver, his most trusted aide in the White House and the man who organized most of the great visual set pieces of the Reagan Presidency, tells how at one crucial moment when deciding to run for major office Reagan said: 'I remember in the movie *Santa Fe Trail* I played George Custer as a young Lieutenant. The Captain said, "You have got to take over" and my line was, "I can't." And the captain said, "But it's your duty". And that's the way I feel about this – I'm going to run.'[4]

Peggy Noonan, one of Reagan's most accomplished speech-writers, confirms that she felt the President made judgements based on movie references. She wrote that: 'For years I had an intuition that his idea of the presidency and how to be president was influenced by a scene in *Yankee Doodle Dandy*, the big hit of 1942.'[5]

Reagan's propaganda advisers, most notably Michael Deaver, approached every issue in entertainment terms. Their most important insight was one they shared with Goebbels – that film (and by extension television) are entertainment media. 'These guys,' Michael Deaver told me, talking of television news journalists, 'they kid themselves they're in the news business. They're not, they're in the entertainment business.'

The impression that the Reagan White House approached politics as entertainment is pervasive. As Lou Cannon writes:

> Over time the cinematic approach became so woven into the fabric of the Reagan presidency that subordinates, schooled in economics or stage craft, routinely used Hollywood terminology to direct Reagan in his daily tasks. One White House aide recalls that Secretary of State George P. Schultz, huddling with Reagen in the secure vault of the American ambassador's residence in Moscow during the 1988 summit, coached him for his meeting with Mikhail Gorbachev by telling him what to do 'in this scene'.[6]

Reagan's ability to turn politics into entertainment was unsurpassed. Details bored him. His basic form of communication was anecdotal. Staff would compete as to who could tell him the funniest story, and at cabinet meetings the President would express himself in anecdotal terms. Every problem was presented as a story, with a beginning, a middle and a punchline. Such a method of communication is significant, because anecdotes can be understood by an eight-year-old whereas analysis cannot. Anecdotes are the enemy of precision. It is impossible to refute an anecdote (unless it claims to be true), only to be amused or bored by it. But anecdotal communication is, of course, the very stuff of entertainment. Comedians tell stories, actors tell stories; and, as President, Reagan conducted the business of the nation by telling stories.

It is not stretching reality to describe the Reagan Presidency as fundamentally an exercise in entertainment. Of course, there were certain 'themes' on which Reagan felt he had been elected, but it was the theatre of the office of state that his propagandists emphasized when they unashamably used Reagan as an actor. 'He was an actor who worked from a script,' said Rhett Dawson, the White House Chief of Operations in the closing years of the Reagan Presidency. 'If you gave him a script he would do it.'[7]

The British experience

The American experience is important in a world context, since entertainment-driven techniques of electronic propaganda have developed there which could only flourish in an unregulated television environment – techniques which are in a sense the 'natural' consequence of the strengths of the medium. But they are not the inevitable consequences.

In Britain, all political propaganda on television is regulated. Politicians cannot simply 'buy' air time – a fact which in America is inconceivable, given the reading that most figures in public life make of the First Amendment to the American constitution which guarantees free speech.

The most important restriction affecting the British propagandist's ability to create emotion-generating, entertainment-led propaganda is the length of airtime permitted for partisan political broadcasts. Thirty-second political adverts are prohibited on British television. Instead, each political party is given a number of ten-minute party political broadcasts – strictly allocated according to the amount of support for each party – for which the airtime is provided free on all networks. The consequences of this simple regulation on the work of British propagandists are enormous.

Sir Tim Bell, Margaret Thatcher's famed 'strategist', confirms that the issue of the length of each party political broadcast is critical. Sitting at his conference table desk, on the top floor of his office building in Mayfair, he told me, 'How can you operate at an emotional level for ten minutes? You might go for the height of emotion for thirty seconds or a minute – maybe two minutes if you've actually got something really good like a murder taking place on screen.' Without a guaranteed murder to raise the emotional tempo of the party political broadcast, British propagandists have reluctantly had to provide actual information in their broadcasts.

Sir Tim, who was influential in Conservative propaganda at every election from 1979 till 1987, came up with a solution to the problem of the ten-minute party politicals – he simply gave some of the time away. A number of senior Conservative politicians told him he was 'out of his mind' to give away television time which was theirs by right, but he remains unrepentant. 'We were trying to make ten-minute broadcasts and the boys kept saying "God, this is hopeless. We can't sustain the argument. We've got to repeat it and repeat it." Whatever technique we were using to try and sustain it for more than five minutes made it very, very difficult.' All Conservative election broadcasts since 1983 with which Bell was involved (with the exception of the leader's final campaign address to the nation) had a duration of five minutes – the Conservatives simply gave away the rest of their allotted time.

But not even Sir Tim Bell had the nerve to give away nine minutes and thirty seconds of his allotted ten minutes, and that is what he would have needed to do for the Conservative party's political propaganda to have rivalled the impact and effectiveness of the emotion-led work of the Americans. It is this necessity to make ten-minute (or at least five-minute) propaganda broadcasts that has resulted in very few British party political broadcasts over the last thirty years being either particularly effective or even particularly memorable. Indeed, in entertainment terms many of them are simply risible, with wooden politicians mouthing tedious statistics.

The American specialist 'TV consultant' has yet to take firm root in British politics. Parties have relied on advice from agencies whose strength and background are in product advertising – from Saatchi's in the case of the Conservatives and a 'shadow communications agency', drawing on the talents of various different advertising people, in the case of Labour. Though the agencies would doubtless eschew the suggestion that they have used methods better suited to advertising, eg, shampoo, others argue that it is for this reason that many of the ten-minute party politicals have been weak. Indeed (until 1992) the only party political broadcast on television that was particularly memorable was the Hugh Hudson film featuring Neil Kinnock transmitted during the 1987 election campaign. It is no surprise that this was biography-type propaganda. As we shall see in chapter 2, biography is one of the few areas of TV political propaganda that can sustain a theme for as long as ten minutes. In the past, too many of the major parties' advisers have made the mistake of trying to concoct ten-minute films about *issues*. Goebbels could have told them that they should never use their time to *inform* the voter. Significantly, it *is* permissible to make thirty- or sixty-second political adverts for the cinema. It is no coincidence that the most effective British political propaganda has been away from TV – like the short cinema advert made by the Saatchis in 1979 entitled *Labour Isn't Working*, which featured a long queue purportedly outside a job centre.

Robbed of thirty-second political commercials – by far the most powerful political weapon in the American propagandist's arsenal – British communicators still have to face up to the reality that their work must compete for attention on television with a mass of programmes that are designed to entertain, not to inform. Sir Tim was the first British propagandist, or 'communicator' as he styles himself, who is generally credited with realising the importance of 'show business' in today's television-driven elections. In 1979 he organized a Conservative youth rally at which a group of celebrities spoke up for Mrs Thatcher. 'The reason showbiz comes into it,' says Bell, 'is that it is much easier to persuade someone with a smile than it is to persuade someone with a frown, and that showbiz is traditionally associated with the idea of pleasure and entertainment and glamour and all those things.'

Although Bell tried to use 'showbiz' and 'showbiz' values in Conservative party propaganda, he faced one other practical political problem which meant that the work he supervised could not approach the emotional intensity of men like Schwartz, Goodman or Slade-White. In Britain, Bell maintains, there is a clear ideological divide between the parties – a divide that is much greater than that between the Republicans and the Democrats in America. As we shall see in Chapter 2, a combination in America of television and money has meant that individual personality is often more important than individual policy in deciding who gets elected. Apart from the care taken over the propaganda portrayal of the leader of the party and his key cabinet or shadow cabinet colleagues, that shift from party to personality has not yet occurred in Britain. Bell believes that on questions like the economy, defence and health, such clear party lines are drawn that propaganda must inevitably deal with issues.

The conventional wisdom in British politics is that an image change was instrumental in the rebuilding of the Labour party in the second half of the 1980s; an image change inspired by, and under the guidance of, former television producer and Director of the party's Communications Peter Mandelson. He was showered with praise for introducing the party's symbol of the red rose, supervising more coherent party political broadcasts and generally making the party 'telegenic'. When I met Mandelson at the London offices of the public relations consultancy where he works part-time in London, he expressed a weary irritation that he was remembered as an 'image'-maker. 'The Tories and the press as much as members of my own party,' he told me, 'have created a myth around me, a sort of Mandelson phenomenon, which is exaggerated, misplaced and slightly barmy in my view.' He believes that both the press and his political opponents have fundamentally missed the point. 'The root causes of the party's credibility problems were to do with policies, were to do with the behaviour of the party. This required a political solution. The leaflets, the party political broadcasts, are wrapping paper – that's icing on the cake. What I always felt, and what Neil

Kinnock believed, was that Labour itself had to be rebuilt – modernized in terms of its policies and appeal.'

In tandem with modernizing the way Labour projected itself on television went a fundamental review of the party's policies – most notably a dropping of the commitment to unilateral disarmament. In Mandelson's view, 'politics is quite different from Persil – you're dealing with complex policies, issues, political tensions and politicians. The whole thing is very much more complex.' As a consequence Mandelson felt that: 'My job was as much as a political manager exercising political judgement and driving things forward politically as it was making sure the set look good, the edit was fine, the hair was in the right place. I left all that to other people.' We must not get carried away, however, with the notion that British politics is in any way immune to entertainment-driven influence. It was Mr Kinnock, after all, who appeared in Tracy Ullman's video in the eighties in order to appeal to younger voters. *Blair on Chris Evans & Brits*

The medium of television is still a vital tool for British propagandists – so much so that experience of TV production is a necessary precondition of appointment as either party's Director of Communications. Shaun Woodward was appointed Conservative Director of Communications in 1991. A major qualification for the job was that he had been a television producer. He had an eye as to how politics should be portrayed on TV – not just the eye of a producer from serious current affairs but the eye of a producer who has also run the most popular consumer programme in Britain, *That's Life*. He frankly admits that it was his television background which made his candidacy so attractive to the party chairman.

One of Woodward's first decisions was to hire John Schlesinger, the British-born Hollywood director, to make a series of party political broadcasts. The first one, transmitted in October 1991, consisted entirely of a series of pretty shots of Britain, using every symbol imaginable – including a baby being born – to show that Britain was better off under the Conservative party. Though the commentary recited a series of statistics cataloguing the claimed successes of the party, the visual imagery used was so strong that no American political consultant would expect the voter really to have listened to what was being said. The broadcast belonged firmly to the 'feel good' school of TV propaganda – a school pioneered by the Americans after Goebbels.

Nor, as we shall see, did both the Conservative party and the Labour party seek the counsel of American TV consultants in the run-up to the 1992 General Election simply because they had nothing else to do with their time. Aspects of American propaganda technique clearly travel across the Atlantic – many of them, as Chapter 2 demonstrates, at the service of the creation of the leader myth.

Notes

1. Boccaccio, G.: *De Genealogia Deorum*, XIV, 9, in *Boccaccio on Poetry*, translated by C.G. Osgood

2. McLuhan, Marshall: *Understanding Media*

3. Cannon, Lou: *President Reagan – The Role of a Lifetime*

4. Deaver, Michael K., with Micky Herskowitz: *Behind the Scenes*

5. Noonan, Peggy: *What I Saw at the Revolution*

6. Cannon, Lou: *President Reagan – The Role of a Lifetime*

7. Ibid

Chapter Two

The Myth of the Leader

No political movement has flourished without a leader. Collectivism may have many theoretical virtues, but in the harsh light of political reality the wise propagandist desires the existence of a strong leader on whom praise can be showered.

The existence of a leader brings many benefits to the propagandist, not least that he can be presented as the personification of his followers' aspirations. In the age when voters took their information from the printed page the leader was inevitably a remote figure, someone whom the ordinary citizen could only read and dream about. The only politicians most people knew personally were their local councillors, Mayor or MP. Film and television changed all that. Now the ordinary citizen could see his leader speak, could 'meet' his family, could form an opinion about his merit based on images which appeared to allow real personal insight. This is why the creation of the leader myth – the presentation of the leader in an idealized form – has become the single most important task in propaganda.

Lessons from the master

More than any other propagandist, Goebbels was the pioneer of visual techniques of myth-making – techniques which are still used by today's political consultants. He knew the propaganda value of a strong leader. In December 1941 Goebbels singled out the creation of the 'Führer Myth' as one of his greatest achievements, and boasted that through it 'Hitler has been given the halo of infallibility'. The Reichsminister realized that he must make the German people believe in Hitler rather than in the Nazi party. Hitler was to become the embodiment of the national values of hope and salvation. He was to become more than a mere man – he was to become the symbol of Germany's regeneration.

The most basic technique used by Goebbels was to exaggerate or even fabricate the qualities which the leader possessed. Hitler was portrayed as a man who had sacrificed himself for the nation – a man of simple tastes, a man who wore a simple uniform, ate simple meals and worked long hours into the night, symbolically watching over the nation. The Führer was shown as a man who had turned his back on normal family life; his celibacy was stressed as yet another sacrifice of his own personal happiness to the happiness of his people (his relationship with Eva Braun was a closely guarded secret).

The extent of the personality cult created around Hitler is evidenced by the introduction of the '*Heil Hitler*' salute, a personal invocation in greeting which elevated Hitler to almost supernatural levels. Goebbels deliberately created around Hitler a messianic aura designed to raise him above the humdrum politics of everyday life. Hitler was always to be portrayed as a man apart. This technique was so successful that during the 1930s Hitler's popularity rose to a much higher level than that of the Nazi party as a whole.

Goebbels realized that the propaganda power of film was so great that the number of appearances made by the Führer had to be carefully controlled, otherwise ordinary Germans might grow too familiar with him. A messiah must be mysterious, never wholly explained. Partially revealing the life of the leader allowed ordinary citizens to participate in the propaganda and supply the rest of the image from their own imagination. This is why, perhaps surprisingly, there was only one feature film made specifically about Hitler – Leni Riefenstahl's *Triumph of the Will*, a record of the party celebrations in Nuremberg in 1934. This film, often thought of as the quintessential Nazi propaganda film, was unusual in many respects. It was commissioned not through Goebbels, but directly by

Hitler who knew Miss Riefenstahl personally. Goebbels did not hide from his close colleagues his feelings about his exclusion. Fritz Hippler recalls, 'Riefenstahl angered Goebbels because it was made possible for her to be creative in films by Hitler personally, so that Goebbels had no say over her whatsoever.' That *Triumph of the Will* is a triumph of propaganda is self-evident, but it did not fit into Goebbels's idea of how the Führer should ideally be portrayed – not least because he had no editorial control over it.

Though Goebbels was careful to say how much he liked *Triumph of the Will* – since the Führer himself admired it, Goebbels would have been foolish to admit anything else – the experiment of a feature-length portrayal of the Führer was not repeated. Instead, Hitler appeared in shorter newsreel reports in a strictly choreographed way. Meeting foreign dignitaries, addressing the party faithful, driving through the flag-lined streets – every appearance of the Führer was carefully stage-managed as much for its filmic effect as for the impression it would create on the actual participants. Such was the attention to detail that those in charge of the newsreels, like Fritz Hippler, were told to try and photograph Hitler from below so that no shadow fell on his moustache. The rallies were pieces of theatre organized for film – a technique that Michael Deaver was later to copy in his presentation of President Reagan's 'photo-opportunities'.

As for the portrayal of the Führer at feature film length, Goebbels preferred a subtler and, inevitably, a more entertaining approach to building the myth than that used by Riefenstahl in *Triumph of the Will*. This was the logic of Goebbels's argument: feature films are best suited to drama, but the Führer's *own* life must not be shown as a drama or else his mystery will disappear. So dramatic films must be made in which the audience can identify with a hero who in some way exhibits Hitler-like qualities. What form should this take? Answer: historical costume dramas about Germany's past.

Propagandists have always tried to link their leaders with past heroes – from the Pope's apostolic succession from St Peter, to Saddam Hussein's imagined familial relationship with Nebuchad-nezzar. Goebbels was one of the first to realize the unique ability of film to create the historical parallel emotionally. He promoted a stream of films about Germany's heroic past – like *Bismarck*, which was released in 1940. Through the personal story of the nineteenth-century statesman who helped unify Germany, Goebbels carefully stressed the necessity for the country to have one man in total control of her destiny, one man standing against the chaos which multi-party democracy would cause. Goebbels intended the audience to make the connection that this was actually a film about the necessity for Germany to have a Hitler.

In a sequel to this film, *Die Entlassung* (*The Dismissal*), released in 1942, Bismarck comes out of retirement to save the nation – and fails. At the end of the film he is made to say, in a less than oblique reference to Hitler, 'My work is done. It was only a beginning – who will complete it?'

The film historian David Welch records a subtler reference to Hitler in connection with the showing of *Der Grosse König* (*The Great King*), a film about Frederick the Great also released in 1942.[1] Goebbels ordered that a shot of Hitler working alone at his desk should be included in the newsreel shown immediately before *Der Grosse König*. The audience would thus see Hitler devoting his every hour to saving Germany and then watch the feature film of Frederick the Great doing just the same; the effect would almost certainly be subliminal – a perfect example of how Goebbels liked his audience not to 'see the art' in his work. Fritz Hippler reveals that 'the German who watched it was supposed to think that here was a similar situation to the present, that the war could be as desperate as that, that there were still possibilities to turn it round and that it could be brought to victory. Frederick the Great was supposed to symbolize Hitler.'

Goebbels realized that the medium of film shifted the focus of government away from the individual local representative and on to the head of state. Now every citizen could feel he had privileged access to the leader. Film could show the office where the leader worked, the country retreat that he went to for solitude, the foreign leaders whom he met. So what the leader looked like became of growing importance. But even Goebbels would not have believed quite how important a politician's physical appearance was going to become with the advent of television.

The look of the leader

If film shifted the focus from the local representative on to the head of state, then the invention of television sharpened that focus still further. If film made the leader accessible to the audience, then the greater intimacy of television made the leader part of the family. Since television allowed the voter to *see* the leader in a way that appeared to humanize him, human qualities like humour and attractiveness became great electoral advantages.

It was in America during the Presidential election of 1956 that, for the first time, the mass electorate of a democratic country could see regularly on TV the competing nominees for the country's greatest office of state. As a result, the one concern that Adlai Stevenson's and General Eisenhower's advisers shared during the campaign was that 'when tilting their heads to read their speeches over television, the candidate's hairless scalps were elongated, suggesting giant eggs'.[2] So, for the first time, baldness became an issue of concern in a Presidential campaign. As Professor Postman says, 'The shape of a man's body is largely irrelevant to the shape of his ideas when he is addressing a public in writing or on the radio, or for that matter in smoke signals. But it is quite relevant on television.'

Television has made the 'look' of the politician vital. Professor Postman believes that the extent to which a President is remembered for his appearance rather than his political acumen has been underestimated. When 'most Americans think of recent Presidents,' says Postman, 'Nixon, Carter or Reagan, the first thing that comes into their mind is their image, how they looked on television. It's instructive to remember that before photography most Americans, if they had to think of Madison or Jefferson or Monroe, would have thought of the words they uttered. Now we think of their images.'

Today's TV consultant wants his candidate to look like a President. But just what does a President look like? In the judgement of veteran Democratic consultant Raymond Strother, he certainly doesn't look like one of the most famous previous incumbents. 'Lincoln didn't look like a President,' says Strother. 'He may have looked like a President a hundred years ago', but he does not look like a President of today. Strother believes that 'Lincoln could never have been elected' in today's TV age. His protruding nose, fleshy lips and sharp chin would have made him fundamentally unappealing to a TV audience. Professor Postman agrees that Lincoln would have had difficulty because 'what was inside his head wouldn't matter as much as what is outside'.

It is not just Lincoln who suffers the indignity of 'not looking like a President'. Professor Postman thinks that 'our twenty-seventh President, William Howard Taft, would be unthinkable even as a candidate in the world of television because he was 327lb, and the grossness of a 327lb image on the television screen would, in all likelihood, overwhelm any articulate sentences that would issue forth from the image's mouth.'

Other evidence supports the view that obesity is a clear disqualification from high office. The New Zealand politician David Lange became Prime Minister in the early 1980s after a stomach operation which reduced his weight from over 300lb to an acceptable 230lb. The medium of television is unforgiving to fat people.

If you find this hard to believe, then next time you are watching the TV news and someone unattractive appears on the screen – someone who is overweight or dishevelled or untidily dressed – ask yourself if you do not make a judgement about them based on their appearance. According to Mark Cook and Robert McHenry, authors of *Sexual Attraction*, you would be abnormal if you did not deduce clues as to a candidate's competence from his looks. Cook and McHenry argue for the existence of 'a strong but often disregarded prejudice against those who are physically unattractive'. They quote analysis of the 1972 Federal elections in Canada, which showed not just that attractive candidates gained a higher percentage of the vote, but that unattractive candidates mostly stood for fringe parties which had little hope of winning. The authors of the study suggested that it might be that 'major parties are conventional in outlook and choose conventionally acceptable i.e. physically attractive candidates', that 'attractiveness helps one advance in any large organisation' and finally that 'the major parties deliberately choose attractive candidates because they think they stand a better chance'.

A politician in a thirty-second commercial is trying to sell himself, and any effective salesman knows the value of looking good. Cook and McHenry confirm that 'physical attraction helps sell goods because so many other socially desirable human attributes are associated with it'. Unattractive people are a rare sight on TV ads. Television as a medium is full of attractive people – often attractive people trying to sell you cars, washing machines or soap powder. The major impact on the voter in such a short timespan (and Cook and McHenry show that the power of physical attractiveness is in first impressions) will be the salesman's physical appearance. Cook and McHenry also reveal that, since prior to the invention of film or television the majority of the population lived in small villages or towns and did not travel much, the ideal standard of 'attractiveness' was lower than it is today. The most attractive man in the village might only be the most attractive man out of fifty people, and the rest of the village had no means of judging him against anyone else. Television changed all that. Now every candidate is judged against the standards of Paul Newman or Warren Beatty.

In America, because of the dominance of TV in the electoral process, the physical appearance of the candidate is of paramount importance; so much so that, as discussed later in this chapter, some candidates gain office who to British eyes seem hardly qualified. But it is a subject that is traditionally whispered about behind the candidate's back. However, not so with TV consultant Raymond Strother. 'There are people who are not electable, and I try to help them through it,' he frankly admits. 'I actually had a candidate one time who came to me and said: "I want to run for office but we'll talk later," and spent about six months in plastic surgery and had his face changed and had suction done on the fat of his body and major operations.'

If the necessity of having major plastic surgery is not enough to put the homely-looking candidate off a political career, then the ultimate fate of Strother's would-be client should be. 'When it was all over, we filmed him,' says Strother, 'and he looked like a nightmare. I took him into the Steenbeck room – the room where we viewed the film – and allowed him to look at himself on television without comment. Twenty-four hours later he called me and told me he was withdrawing from the race.'

In Strother's view plastic surgery made this potential candidate 'look worse' than before. 'There was some trick the camera played on him and I'm not sure what it was. It made him look very feminine. If

he were in the room with you, you couldn't tell it. But on camera –
the camera was very cruel to him.'

Who is to say what cruel tricks the camera might have played on
Abraham Lincoln or Howard Taft or even George Washington?
And if none of the above 'looks' like a President, then who does?
Raymond Strother is in no doubt: 'My ideal candidate probably
would look like Gary Hart.' Strother was Hart's political consultant
in the 1984 Presidential campaign. 'I thought he was the perfect
man,' says Strother. 'You want them to represent sort of a
Mid-Western accent and style. They can't be too regional. They
can't be too southern. They can't be too western.' Hart had one other
vital advantage. 'He was a handsome, striking man and people were
drawn to him physically. Gary Hart looked like a President. He
looked like a candidate should look.'

Strother believes there has been a fundamental change in the
appearance of American politicians since the invention of television.
'Image is very important,' he says. 'If you had a yearbook of the US
Senate from thirty or forty years ago you'd find a lot of unappealing,
unattractive people. If you had a yearbook of people elected in the
last ten years you'd find a whole group of attractive people.'

Strother is not alone in stressing the importance of the candidate's
physical appearance. Almost every TV consultant I spoke to said
that conventional good looks were an advantage, and specifically
that their ideal candidate would be neither fat nor bald. These
consultants do not say such things lightly. They realize that the
candidate has to compete for attention on television amongst a
variety of other TV performers who are themselves, to a varying
degree, chosen for their looks.

One class of TV performer more than any other influences the
'look' of the modern candidate. In the words of Peggy Noonan, one
of President Reagan's speech-writers: 'At the end of the Reagan era,
all the Presidential candidates looked like TV news guys.'

But why should the physical appearance and the deportment of
the news 'anchorman' be the standard by which the American voter
judges the candidate? Because anchormen are trusted figures in
American society; they are the men (and on the major evening
network news there are seldom any women) who look Americans
straight in the eye and tell them the truth – and they are believed.

55

We all take the fame of the 'anchor' for granted, but in another age it would have seemed incredible that, in the words of Joe McGinniss, 'we make celebrities not only of the men who cause events but of the men who read reports of them aloud'.[3]

A television fiction is created around the 'anchor': that he is all-knowledgeable about domestic politics and world affairs, that he can offer both spontaneous wry wit and sincere judgement. It is a fiction which the tens (in some cases hundreds) of TV professionals involved in the news conspire to project. For the TV anchor is in reality the public face of a huge news-gathering operation. Editorial judgement is actually exercised by many others.

Nowhere in television is the perceived gap in influence between those who appear in front of the camera and those who work behind it wider than in the newsroom. Physically the programme producers are feet away from the anchor, but in the audience's perception they might as well be on the moon. Just such a phenomenon is occurring within politics. 'More and more the candidate was the front man,' observes Peggy Noonan. 'More and more he was just the talker. Our Senate and our House candidates, even some of our presidential candidates are becoming like anchormen.'[4]

Such sentiments might be perceived as radical, because it is in the interests of neither the TV consultant nor of the candidate to be wholly frank about the importance of the candidate's 'look' or the influence of his TV consultant. A candidate who speaks openly would lay himself bare to the charge that he was simply a good-looking 'puppet'. Yet a few politicians *have* admitted how much television has changed them. One of the most honest, in this if nothing else, is Richard Nixon, the man who is traditionally credited as being the first candidate to learn the hard way the lesson that on TV physical appearance matters. He lost considerable ground in the 1960 Presidential election because he looked sweaty and unsure during his first TV debate with John F. Kennedy; this was later ascribed to a slight knee injury and Nixon's refusal to wear make-up. He never forgot the lessons of the 1960 campaign.

'Rely totally on your television producer,' Nixon subsequently advised other candidates, 'let him put make-up on you even though you hate it, let him tell you how to sit, let him tell you what your best camera angles are, let him tell you what to do with your hair – it must turn people off to think that you've got to go to the barber and get your hair blown dry and then fixed just properly and everything in place, but that's the television age. It turns me off, I hate to do it, but having been burned once by not doing it I never made that mistake again and I would urge all prospective candidates in the future, be sure to remember that more important than what you say is how you look on television.'[5]

Nixon realized the truth of Joe McGinniss's statement: 'The TV candidate, then, is not measured against his predecessors – not against a standard of performance established by two centuries of democracy – but against Mike Douglas.'

The myth of autobiography

Once today's TV propagandist has convinced his candidate of the importance of the correct appearance (from having his hair cut to his jawline altered), the next stage in the creation of the leader myth is to demonstrate the candidate's extraordinary qualities of political leadership. In the past this might have been done by the candidate espousing certain policies or by showing his detailed grasp of the great issues facing the nation; but today's TV propagandist has found a simpler and safer route to raise perception of the candidate's ability. The secret is autobiography. Television loves personalities and stories; autobiography combines the two.

Television's predisposition for telling the candidate's life story is a natural consequence of the medium's ability to make the viewers feel that they are on intimate terms with TV personalities. The voters see personalities and politicians on their screens every day; they are welcome guests in their living rooms, people in whose company hours, often years, are spent. What could be more natural than to want to learn their history? As the *Washington Post*'s Paul Taylor observed, 'Men win nominations now on the steadiness of their step and the soundness of their autobiographies . . . As candidates made biography the heart of their campaigns, the voters perked up and paid attention. They liked the stories; they related to them.'

The format into which the candidate's autobiography is squeezed is normally the thirty-second (occasionally the sixty-second) TV commercial. In this impressionistic arena modesty and self-deprecating humour are the order of the day, not just if the candidate is appearing himself, but also if his family are vouching for him. One of the most skilful of recent autobiographical 'endorsement' ads on US television was made by Joe Slade-White for an incumbent candidate for the governorship of Oregon. An old man sits on a bench and says, 'Some people say Neil Goldschmidt is a big spender, but I happen to know that Neil Goldschmidt was taught about money by one of the toughest economists in this state.' The picture widens to show a grey-haired, smiling lady. 'His Mom.'

A definite plus for the candidate is a good war record. In a 1980 ad for Bush's Presidential campaign Robert Goodman showed archive film of the young George Bush emerging from the Pacific on to an American submarine after his plane had been shot down. The ad successfully demonstrated Bush's unexpected 'macho' credentials. Time spent in action in Vietnam is even more valuable to today's propagandist. If the candidate is a Republican it shows he did not take the 'Quayle' option and stay at home; if a Democrat, it protects him from suspicions about his patriotism.

Dealing with the past not only intrigues the audience since it is the background story of a celebrity; it has an additional advantage – it can't be contradicted. Unless, of course, the candidate *invents* his autobiography. This is not unknown. In a recent governorship campaign in Kentucky one of the candidates gave the 'impression' he had served in the fifties in the US Army in the Korean war. He was later revealed to have served in Japan. His luckless TV consultant was forced to weasel, 'My candidate meant he served in the Korean war *area* – that includes Japan, doesn't it?'

The candidate's autobiography should be sufficiently flexible to adapt to the weaknesses of his opponent. When he stood in the wake of Watergate, Jimmy Carter's propagandists represented him as an 'honest businessman'. When he stood in 1980 against Edward Kennedy for the Democratic party's nomination, his propagandists portrayed him as 'Husband, Father, President,' before adding portentously: 'He's done these three jobs with distinction.' The aim here was to contrast Carter's happy domestic life with Kennedy's troubled one, without going as far as to mention directly any of his rival's personal flaws. Attack and autobiography should never be mixed. If your opponent is perceived as a coward, then it is enough to stress your own bravery and leave it to the voter to make the comparison. Autobiographical propaganda belongs firmly to the 'feel good' school of TV persuasion.

If the candidate is standing for re-election, then the propagandist's ability to create the leader myth is greatly helped – not least by the fact that an incumbent President can always get himself on television when his advisers want him to. A President who seeks re-election will often be portrayed not as another candidate but as 'The President'. This technique, reminiscent of the way Goebbels projected Hitler, was the central strategy of the Nixon re-election campaign in 1972. The idea was that Nixon would be 'positioned' as above the fray; Spiro Agnew, his Vice-President, could do battle with George McGovern, the Democratic challenger, but Nixon would be shown only in a 'Presidential stance'.

Other advantages of incumbency include the Presidential props. The White House, the Oval Office, Camp David, Air Force One – all can be pressed into service. It is important that a President seeking re-election should be shown doing things that only a President can do in places only a President could be – conferring with world leaders is a popular option. One analyst believes that a major fault Gerald Ford made in the 1976 campaign was in allowing himself to be portrayed on the nightly news as a candidate, whilst his Secretary of State, Henry Kissinger, stole his limelight by being shown as a statesman in Europe and the Middle East.

Since the challenger does not have the opportunity to use the President's props of office, a common alternative is to be seen as somehow 'trying on' the mantle of office. Carter successfully managed this trick in his 1976 campaign when talking of his 'vision' of America. As Robert Spero saw it, 'Jimmy Carter's genius lay in his ability to pre-empt for himself those qualities that Pollster Pat Caddell found people craved the most: honesty above all else, followed by honesty's political bedfellows: trust, reliability, goodness, caring, responsiveness and – perhaps for the first time in American political history – love.'[6] Professor Jamieson agrees that Carter 'invited voters to see his presidency as the realization of his dreams and aspirations – whatever they might be.'[7]

The wise propagandist does not limit his candidate's 'trying on' of the Presidency just to words. In his 1980 campaign for George Bush, Robert Goodman employed actors to pose as secret service men around the candidate. The proximity of film crews and journalists is also a sure visual mark of status – though today even genuine film crews can be misconstrued by cynical politicians. In 1989 I was making a film for BBC TV about Lord King, chairman of British Airways and friend of Mrs Thatcher's. We were filming him at the BA reception at the Conservative party conference, following him around in a *cinéma vérité* style. 'Look at King,' I heard one Conservative MP say to another. 'That man's ego is so huge that he's hired a film crew for the evening just to follow him around.'

Propagandists are well aware that the TV audience makes judgements based on visual clues: which car the candidate is driven in, how many film crews are around him, the number of microphones in front of him when he speaks. These are not mere details – they are some of the very bricks with which the leader myth is built. The higher the status of the politician, the more his awareness of the power of the visual cue. Bob Gates, now Director of the CIA but until recently Deputy US Secretary of State, revealed that he was concerned by the visual impression he and James Baker gave when they arrived at Alexandria airport in Egypt to confer with President Hosni Mubarak during the Gulf crisis. They arrived in a small twin-propeller plane whilst the Iraqi delegation had turned up in a massive passenger jet. Trivial? Not to the Americans, anxious to portray their country as strong and ready for battle.[8]

How to film the leader

Twenty years ago the *cinéma vérité* style of filming was very much in vogue. Distinguished documentary maker Charles Guggenheim used this technique – in which the camera is often hand-held and action is filmed unplanned, 'as it happens' – in his work for George McGovern's Presidential campaign against Nixon in 1972. The advantage was that the candidate was seen in a naturalistic way interacting with the voters. Such ads have a 'high risk' feel to them, with the viewers thinking they are watching something unstaged and therefore exciting. The problem is that, while the candidate looks active, he rarely looks Presidential. This was certainly McGovern's problem in 1972: the *vérité* technique played into the hands of Nixon's propagadists, who were busy showing the incumbent Nixon as 'The President' and thus above the hurly-burly of battle.

In the 1976 primaries against Gerald Ford, Ronald Reagan also became to some extent the victim of the *vérité* technique. His propagandists had decided that they must not play on Reagan's background as an actor, so they decided to show him in a variety of *vérité* situations – mingling with voters and so on. It didn't work, because Reagan's strength was precisely that he *was* an actor. When the campaign reached the Southern states, the TV technique changed and Reagan started speaking direct to camera in a controlled way which played to his acting abilities – it worked. Reagan won the very next primary.

The propagandist must be aware that television audiences are capricious and no single technique works for ever. Today the technique of the leader talking direct to camera is going out of fashion. The 'focus groups' (a selection of average voters who give their views on each ad to the consultant before the commercials are shown on TV) are telling the consultants that it simply isn't effective. In the words of Dayne Strother, Ray's son, 'The problem is that American politicians have for so long looked into the camera and made promises that they're not believable any more.' One of the masters of the 'looking to camera, act sincere' technique was one of the Strother family's clients, ex-Governor of Louisiana Buddy Roemer. Dayne describes Roemer as a candidate who could 'sell a man with no teeth two steaks' and as 'the last guy who could promise what he'd do on camera and they [the voters] would think he could deliver'.

Partly because voters felt politicians like Roemer did not 'deliver', Dayne Strother has changed his technique of filming candidates and now shows them 'in action', with an announcer voicing their achievements over the picture. Despite this technique Buddy Roemer (whom Dayne Strother described as 'an android to a degree') lost the Republican nomination for Governor in the 1991 Louisiana primaries to the neo-Nazi David Duke.

The current fashionable technique seems to be to allow the candidate to speak to camera only so long as he is not actually promising anything, and then to film him in action in a variety of controlled situations using commentary to list his achievements. But even this method may shortly be passé. The future is probably best seen in some of the autobiographical ads made by the New York-based Democratic consultant, Joe Slade-White, which have shown that words can be superfluous. One of his ads for Neil Goldschmidt, campaigning for re-election as Governor of Oregon in 1986, shows a swift series of vignettes of the candidate: holding a meeting and acting decisive, pacing down a corridor, taking calls from constituents and working late into the night at his desk. Each scene is separated from another by captions with messages like 'It's about work' and 'It's about change', ending with a caption reading 'It's about time'. Exciting music with a firm, catchy beat is all that is heard on the soundtrack.

Television techniques to project the leader myth have come a long way in the last thirty-five years, from Adlai Stevenson interminably reading his speeches to camera in 1956 to Slade-White's candidate for the governorship of Oregon who doesn't have a word to say to his electorate in his ad. Without words, the candidate's acting ability and looks become all-important – indeed, they become the *only* political message that is promoted.

The vital personal quality

There is another quality which the propagandist must instil in the candidate that is more important than any previously discussed – a quality which Roger Ailes calls 'the magic bullet'. What is it? Is it a grasp of policy, an understanding of the problems facing the great nation of America? No. In Roger Ailes's words: 'it is the quality of being likeable . . . if your audience likes you, they'll forgive you just about everything else you do wrong. If they don't like you, you can hit every rule right on target and it doesn't matter.'[9]

Above all else the leader must strive continually for what Ailes calls a high 'like quotient'. American TV consultants realize that since voters draw their values from television, they will apply television criteria to judging the candidate. They will judge the candidate as they will judge Dan Rather or Johnny Carson or

Batman. And they are guaranteed to ask themselves one question: 'Do I like him?' Joe McGinniss spotted the consequence of this trend during the Nixon campaign in 1968, when he wrote, 'Television seems particularly useful to the politician who can be charming but lacks ideas. Print is for ideas.'[10] Nixon's propagandists knew this truth as well, just as much as they knew they were landed with a potentially unlikeable candidate. An internal memo written by one of Nixon's communication team in 1968 suggests that Nixon should attempt to show 'human warmth', by not answering every question so perfectly and be seen occasionally 'groping for an answer'.

There is a remarkable consensus among TV consultants on the need for a high 'like quotient' in their candidate. Raymond Strother puts it this way: 'People elect people. They don't elect issues. They don't like positions on issues. They like people. And what they want to do is look someone in the eye – on television if need be – and say "I like him".' Strother, a consultant about as far removed politically from Ailes as it is possible to get, nonetheless agrees with the Republican that to make the voter 'like' the candidate is the 'single most important thing' the consultant can achieve.

How does a candidate achieve a high 'like quotient'? Ailes has the answer. 'People who are unlikeable complain about their problems, jabber constantly about meaningless things, and talk in a monotone. They are overly serious and rarely smile or joke about anything.' Likeable people are 'optimistic' and 'genuinely concerned about the well-being of other people'. They use humour to defuse difficult situations. Ailes concludes his dissertation on likeability in his book *You Are the Message* with the wistful thought, 'I've often thought that if people would just go a little out of their way to help others, there'd be no problem with anybody's like quotient'. The informed reader may have a little trouble with Ailes's piety, since he is known as the roughest and toughest political consultant around, the man behind the furlough ad which led to the controversy over Willie Horton at the 1988 American Presidential election (see page 105), the man who bullies his candidates, and who was reported in *Newsweek* as having instructed his client George Bush during a coaching session to 'stop waving your fucking hands, you look like a goddam pansy'.

One President who had no problem with his 'like quotient' was

Ronald Reagan. Indeed, the most remarkable fact about his Presidency is not that an actor became President, but that such a *nice* actor became President. Tip O'Neill, one of Reagan's fiercest political opponents, said simply, 'You know, I like the man.' Reagan was the personification of the qualities which Ailes demands in a 'likeable' candidate. He was optimistic – so incredibly optimistic that every single night he would go to bed believing that tomorrow would be an even better day. He was considerate of the feelings of others: 'You always got the impression that he felt it was a privilege to meet you,' writes Peggy Noonan. Above all, he had a sense of humour. He was probably the funniest man ever to become President, with a nice line in self-deprecatory jokes. 'It's true hard work never killed anyone,' was one of his most famous one-liners, 'but I figure – why take the chance?' His humour supported those around him at moments of great stress. After he was shot, as he lay in his hospital bed, he jotted down a note which read: 'I'd like to do that scene again, starting at the hotel.'

Since Reagan was an entertaining, attractive figure, someone for whom the medium of television might have been invented, there exists the possibility that the American people might have been electing a man they liked, but a politician whose policies they disliked. Professor Postman puts it this way: 'I have no quarrel with someone who voted for Reagan who also believed, let's say, in supply side economics [non-interventionist, market-led policies]. The problem comes when people do not agree with that, see that in fact such a policy is injurious to their own economic self-interest and vote for him anyway because he's likeable. That makes, it seems to me, a new conception of politics – a mockery of an older view of politics.' Postman had specific experience of this 'liking the man, hating his policies' phenomenon when he talked to some farmers during the 1984 Reagan re-election campaign. 'It was pretty clear that Reagan's policies would be injurious to them,' says Postman, who went on to ask: '"Well, why did you vote for Reagan, or why do you plan to vote for him?" And they would say, "Well, he's so nice, and I like him and I trust him" and I'd say, "But you have four years of evidence that his policies are not suitable to your own interests." This is irrational.'

Postman believes that: 'Television so intensifies and amplifies the irrational element in politics that it becomes difficult to find any piece that's rational.' He concludes: 'I don't know that it's necessary for us to have political leaders we like. I think we would be better off with political leaders that we regard as intelligent and who have, or will, pursue policies that reflect our own economic and sociological interests.'

Most American TV consultants dismiss Postman's views. Their attitude can be summarized like this: politics is conducted on television – that's a fact. One consequence of this fact is that the candidate will be judged on much more personal criteria than ever before – what he looks like, what his personal story is, above all, whether he's a likeable sort of guy. There's no point in moaning about it. It's just the way it is.

But the logical conclusion of such a sanguine view is that it is possible that a voter might both like someone, and know that he is totally unsuited for office in terms of ability, experience and personal character – yet still vote for him. Incredible? It's already happening in the third world, as Chapter 7 demonstrates.

The essential prerequisite

We have established that a candidate must look Presidential, he must sound Presidential, he must act Presidential, he must be filmed in a modern Presidential way. Above all he must be likeable. But we have omitted the most important precondition of all. Money.

It is essential that the candidate have access to large quantities of dollars. Every consultant interviewed for this book stressed the importance of money. Jim Duffy put it best when he said, 'Of the five most important things the candidate needs, one two and three are money.' Without money there is no campaign, because all political ads (except for a complicated subsidy during Presidential campaigns) have to be paid for. Airtime is not free to political parties in America as it is in England, and the consequences are profound. Duffy is resigned to the problem. 'This is a country that's based on money,' he says. 'It's based on acquisitiveness. Many times we judge success or failure by whether you raise money or don't raise money.'

Consultants expect to be paid for their work. As Frank Luntz, one of the youngest of them, puts it, 'If I were to be totally candid, a lot of consultants don't necessarily work with people who propagate their point of view. They work with people with a large cheque book.' So what is the consequence of this reliance on money? According to Raymond Strother, it's obvious. 'I hate to say it, but poor people can't get elected now. How does someone get elected in America if television's the single most important thing and you must purchase it?' Some consultants say that poor people should go out and raise money from rich friends, but as Strother aptly says, 'If you're really poor you probably don't have friends who are really rich because rich people have rich friends. So what you find, in the Senate particularly, is a group of very rich men.'

The result of all this is a fundamental problem for the American democratic system. 'Some of our best and brightest now aren't being elected to office,' says Strother. 'It's a great danger to us all that there are people out there – business people, academics, people who would serve well – who know they don't have a chance in hell of being elected. So they don't run. Or they come to somebody like me and they say, "What do I need to run?" and I say "Bring a million dollars, and then you can run, but if you can't get that, don't run."' Strother reveals that a man with 'all sorts of credentials' came to him and said he wanted to stand for election as Governor of Alabama. This prospective candidate had many academic qualifications and had been a senior legal figure in the state, but he couldn't raise the necessary money to fund his campaign so he went to Strother and asked for his advice. Strother said, 'You should quit', and so in the consultant's view 'a lesser person is Governor of Alabama' as a consequence.

Frank Greer is another TV consultant in no doubt about the importance of money in the electoral process. 'Fundamentally I think what's wrong with American politics is that it's got too expensive.' Greer, one of the most successful of Democratic consultants, disagrees with his colleagues who protect the status quo by maintaining that the ability of the candidate to raise large amounts of money represents some sort of test of the candidate's organizational ability and is therefore, in a way, a test of his leadership ability. Greer speaks plainly about where the bulk of the money to run a campaign has to come from. 'We are dependent on special interest groups to raise the money', and America therefore ends up with 'government that serves the interests of whoever's got a lot of money'. Raising the money from special interest groups brings with it one big problem – that group is going to want the candidate, once he is in office, to do something special in their interest.

Greer believes America is at the point 'where there is paralysis in Congress. People are afraid to take bold stands in favour of the public interest because they have to raise money from special interest. From big corporations. From big unions. And they have to have that money because campaigns are so expensive.' Greer points specifically to health care as an issue that has been affected by the politician's need to take money from special interest groups. 'Here in Washington no one will take a position for health care simply because they don't want to offend the doctors or the hospitals or the insurance companies or whatever it may be. So we end up with a terrible health care system and 30 million people uninsured, which would be unheard of in England or any other European country. But the reason we don't have health care in this country is because advertising and television and the way we run campaigns means that candidates are afraid to take a bold position in public.'

The perfect candidate

With all this information, all these secrets from today's propagandists, we are now in a position to construct the perfect candidate to fulfil the leader myth. The first thing we can say about our candidate is that he is a man. A woman, according to Dottie Lynch, now political editor of CBS News but a former political pollster, has difficulties passing the test of the 'polls'. 'Women were criticized' in polls, she says, 'or talked about in terms of their looks much more than male candidates.' Plus, as Raymond Strother says dismissively, 'Women have trouble raising money – that's why there aren't more women in Congress.'

So our ideal candidate is a man – a man, furthermore, who is good-looking and probably looks rather like Gary Hart. He is either rich himself or has rich friends. He is likeable and inoffensive, and he tells good jokes – often self-deprecating ones. Our candidate need not be especially gifted intellectually – Reagan certainly wasn't. So who would be our ideal candidate? Why, J. Danforth Quayle, of course. Quayle is good-looking (often compared in appearance to Robert Redford), he comes from one of the richest families in Indiana, and he always does his best to have a high 'like quotient'. Roger Ailes was rumoured to have been instrumental in George Bush choosing Quayle as his running mate, and it is not hard to see why Ailes picked him – he passes every modern propaganda test. After all, no one ever said that excessive political competence was one of the selection criteria. So the logic of all this is that no one should have been remotely surprised that Dan Quayle was nominated for Vice-President of the United States, and this despite the fact that the press subsequently attacked him for being politically inept and intellectually barren. Quayle is still a heartbeat away from the Presidency – a rich, good-looking, rather dim man who has leapt ahead of his political contemporaries because of his suitability for the medium of television. His career is a triumph of propaganda over political distinction. In fact, we ought to be surprised that there are not more Dan Quayles.

The story of the 1988 election of W. Gaston Caperton as Governor of West Virginia shows that the analysis of the ideal candidate is correct. Frank Greer was sitting in his office on Pennsylvania Avenue in Washington one day in the summer of 1987 when he got a call from a man he had never heard of – Gaston Caperton. Greer had been recommended to him by several of his 'business associates' as the sharpest political consultant in town. Caperton explained that he wanted to become Governor of West Virginia. He had no previous political experience and was standing against four state-wide office holders, people who had been in public life for some time. Caperton was currently standing at 3 per cent in the polls – a statistic that Greer felt, on examination, probably exaggerated the candidate's support. Greer heard all this and was none the less enthusiastic, for Caperton had said the magic words: 'I can write a cheque for this campaign.' His family ran a large insurance business and he was a very rich man indeed.

When Greer actually met Caperton he must have been even more enthusiastic, for Caperton is no Abraham Lincoln look-alike. He is slim, with a good head of hair and nice teeth. He looks just as a young, thrusting Governor should in this TV age. Admittedly Caperton had some disadvantages, such as the fact that he had never appeared in front of a camera or 'given a big speech'. But problems like these could be solved, whilst a combination of lack of money and lack of looks would have proved terminal.

Greer took Caperton up from 3 per cent in the polls to a position where he went on to win his primary by 10 per cent and to defeat the incumbent Governor by 20 per cent. Greer is frank about how this was achieved. 'The fact of the matter was that Gaston Caperton spent several million dollars on the air and we outspent our opponents.' The consultant was fortunate enough to work for a candidate who had 'more resources to commit' than anyone else in the race.

It would be unfair to say that Gaston Caperton simply bought the governorship. His propaganda was slick, for Greer is a talented consultant. The ads showed him against a variety of backgrounds – meeting teachers, meeting hard-hatted workmen – all in poses of authority. The candidate looked sincerely to camera and mouthed his platitudes well.

Greer is defensive about the lack of political content in the ads. He says that Caperton did have a programme of policies and that this programme was lodged in libraries in case anyone wanted to read it. This is symbolic of the American TV age. The candidate hides his actual proposals away so that only a tiny percentage of the electorate will read them, whilst his ads, which everyone sees, concentrate on the most important propaganda policy of all – the policy of making the voter like the look of the candidate.

Caperton was aided by the fact that the 'free' media – newspapers and the TV news – traditionally play less of a part in an election at state level than they do at Federal or Presidential level. The chances are that the Gaston Capertons of this world are much less likely to receive the sort of scrutiny that national candidates like Michael Dukakis have to endure.

In the end the most damning statistic of the Caperton campaign has, not surprisingly, to do with money. Greer estimates that Caperton probably spent $2.5 million in the primary and another $1.5–2 million in the general election, a total of around $5 million to win the job of Governor of West Virginia – a job which carries an annual salary of around $70,000.

Beware of dissonance

In democratic countries newspaper and TV journalists may choose not just to report the image of the candidate that is offered by the TV propagandist. They may decide to do some investigation of their own. The main way in which the 'free' media try to undermine the leader myth is by showing a disparity between the image which is created on the 'paid' element of the propagandist's campaign – the TV ads – and the way the candidate appears on the 'free' side – primarily the nightly news. As we shall see in Chapter 5, there are a number of detailed ways in which the propagandist tries to manipulate the nightly TV news; but there are in addition several techniques which the propagandist can use specifically to deflect investigation of the leader.

The first is simple. Don't let the press have access to the candidate. This can only really be practised by propagandists working for incumbent politicians. The excuse that the candidate cannot talk because of a busy schedule involving matters of state or because of 'security' problems only works as long as the propagandist's client is in office.

At some point the candidate is going to meet the press. If the resultant reports are positive, they carry the added advantage of an 'independent third party endorsement'. But the journalist is generally out of the propagandist's control, and the main difficulty arises if the journalist discovers that the candidate is not the same person that the ads say he is. One of the commercials in Edward Kennedy's 1980 campaign showed him walking along a beach with his family whilst the commentary said, 'The kinds of things he has suffered have made him a strong, more mature, man.' It didn't work. The viewer knew that the image of Kennedy as a happily married, wiser man was inconsistent with the image painted in the 'free' press of Kennedy as a hard-drinking womanizer.

As experienced Southern TV consultant Jim Duffy puts it, the problem crops up when 'it becomes painfully apparent that we have created something over here that is radically different from what they see over there'. Duffy believes the 'classic' example of this was the campaign of Clayton Williams, who ran for Governor of Texas in 1990. His consultant created what Duffy calls: 'Beautiful television, wonderful television'. But 'as the campaign wore on for about a year the difference between his TV spots and the image that was created with what they saw in the free media was the difference between something that was totally contrived and something that wasn't – and he should have won easily in a Conservative state.' The difficulty was that the candidate 'kept saying outrageous things. The more they interviewed him, the more it was apparent that he didn't know how governments work, and so he was just literally shooting himself in the foot daily. I mean here's a guy who ended the campaign with no toes. He shot them all off. It's amazing he could walk.'

A propagandist who realizes that his candidate has a secret at odds with the image created by his television ads has few choices. 'It's our job to present the best possible image of a candidate. Hide his flaws. I admit that,' says Raymond Strother, a man who believes that the better the consultant the longer it takes the voter to 'detect the flaws' in the candidate. Strother believes that to get a 'flawed' candidate elected 'there are two things you can do. Run a very short campaign. Run a one-month campaign – or a three-week campaign – and inundate people with favourable information and get the election finished before they've found the truth out. That's one way to do it, and the other way to do it would be to run a long, long campaign and pray and hope that people won't find out some of the flaws in the candidate.'

Strother, it should be remembered, was the campaign manager of Gary Hart, so he should have learned a thing or two about the importance of concealing a candidate's flaws. He still believes that Hart would have made a fine President, and is disappointed by his candidate's fall as a result of allegations of sexual indiscretion. 'The rules have changed in America,' says Strother. 'When I began this business in 1965 there was sort of a gentleman's agreement that we didn't talk about mistresses or girlfriends or sexual proclivities. We had an agreement we didn't do that because that was human, and we winked at each other. The rules changed. It came about the time that women came into journalism in large numbers and they were more personal than men in the way they judged candidates.'

There is, however, another explanation for the media's fascination with the personal life of the candidate. American morals can hardly have changed substantially since the days when adulterers like Roosevelt, Eisenhower and Kennedy were in the White House, all of whom escaped office with their honour untarnished. But none of them were *television* Presidents, none of them were exposed to the sort of TV coverage which all of today's Presidential contenders either endure or enjoy. The illusion is created that the voter knows the candidate intimately, especially since TV consultants concentrate more on the candidate's autobiography than on his policies. The result is that the voters are much more curious about the personal lives of Gary Hart or Bill Clinton than they were about the personal lives of Franklin D. Roosevelt or Dwight D. Eisenhower. Television has spawned an electoral system which prefers gossip to issues.

The British system

Two fundamental differences between the British and American political systems affect the way the leader myth is constructed on this side of the Atlantic. First, in Britain only the leader's own constituents vote for him directly; everyone else votes for his or her own individual MP, who in turn influences the choice of leader. Second, money cannot buy you either political airtime or elective office.

Since the Prime Minister is not directly elected by the voters it is less important that a high 'like quotient' be created around the leader's personality. Indeed, in Britain in the 1980s the reverse of the Reagan phenomenon occurred. Some voters elected Reagan because they disliked his policies but liked the man; some voters voted for Thatcher, though they disliked the woman, because they liked her policies.

Similarly, it would do you little good to turn up to a Conservative party preliminary candidate selection meeting, held at a motel near London every few months, and offer £1 million to become a candidate. Money would do you even less good in your attempt to become a Labour MP. Selection is stated to be on perceived political merit.

But none of this means that the British propagandist can ignore the importance of the leader myth. A popular leader can pull a party up in the polls just as an unpopular one can drag a party down, and British politicians are just as aware of the importance of television popularity as are their American counterparts. But there are differences of approach between the two countries. Take the question of physical appearance. At first sight it does not appear to be important for a British politician to be good-looking. Sir Tim Bell, Mrs Thatcher's most trusted 'political communications' adviser throughout the eighties, dismisses the importance of looks: 'It's crap,' he says simply. He points to figures like the former Liberal Democrat MP Cyril Smith and the former Conservative Chancellor of the Exchequer Nigel Lawson as examples of fat yet successful politicians. But is he right to be so dismissive? Three years ago the Liberal Democrats selected a new leader for their party. The choice was effectively between Alan Beith, the deputy leader of the party, and Paddy Ashdown, the party's spokesman on education and science. Beith was the more experienced and (to be blunt) probably the more intelligent. Ashdown was the better-looking – something that was referred to by commentators at the time as 'more charismatic'. The leader of the Liberal Democrats is unique amongst the leaders of the main parties in that he or she is elected solely by the membership at large. Isn't it possible that the membership, who will have received most of their information about the candidates from television, simply acted as many American consultants would have predicted, and voted for the better-looking candidate? Remember that the last leader to be elected in such a way was Dr David Owen, the leader of the Social Democratic Party, whose matinee-idol good looks were for a long time the subject of comment by columnists in the popular papers.

This is a fraught area for any political analysis since there is little possibility of voters admitting openly that they are influenced by looks; by clothes – possibly. Michael Foot's appearance at the annual Remembrance Day celebrations in a duffle coat, when leader of the Labour party, was seen as worthy of legitimate criticism on the grounds of 'disrespect'; but it is rare for anyone in Britain to declare openly that they vote on the basis of looks. It is even rarer in Britain than in America for a politician frankly to admit the importance of the propagandist's advice, especially in the way it relates to television. One of the first statements John Major made on being elected to the leadership of the Conservative party was to declare that the 'image' makers would not change him. As Joe McGinniss noted, the candidate should 'express distaste for television; suspicion that there is something phoney about it. This guarantees him good press, because newspaper reporters, bitter over their loss of privilege to the television men, are certain to stress the anti-television remarks.'

Nor is it in the interests of the British propagandist to stress his *own* importance – after all, he relies on business from his clients, and his clients are politicians who would not take kindly to credit being snatched from their own hands. Yet the fact is that propagandists on both sides of the Atlantic do have great influence. One can judge this both from the political reality and from the sort of remarks the propagandists – particularly the American ones – make when they talk 'off the record'. One said to me, 'Frankly, give me twenty million dollars and I can get a brick elected.' Now, no one is saying that the British propagandist could get a brick elected to the House of Commons, but only a naive politician would not listen to the advice of his television expert, and there are few naive politicians who survive in Parliament for long.

Accepting that one cannot necessarily take at face value either the protestations of the politicians that they are immune from 'image' making advice or the open statement from many 'image' makers that they are of limited influence, what do the facts say? It is a fact, for instance, that Mrs Thatcher changed her appearance after Sir Gordon Reece, a former television producer, appeared on the scene as Director of Communications of the Conservative party in 1978.[11] Shortly after Reece began his work, the *Daily Telegraph* noticed: 'There has been something intriguingly professional about the panache and growing confidence of Mrs Thatcher's public appearances.' Reece has always denied that he personally demanded that Mrs Thatcher's hair be redone (though it is a fact that it was), or that her voice became softer (though it is a fact that it did). Maybe Mrs Thatcher spontaneously thought of these changes herself at the same time as Reece, a man in whose judgement she had great trust, assumed his new role. But whoever decided on Thatcher's change in appearance, a change in appearance there undeniably was, and one that any American TV consultant would say was a change for the better as far as her TV image was concerned.

Nor have Labour party leaders been immune from the attempts of their advisers to pretty them up. After Harold Wilson became leader of the Labour party not only did he have his teeth fixed, but during the 1973 election a make-up man called George Blackler who had worked on Hammer Horror films was brought in to travel on the election campaign with him. Wilson's adviser, Lady Falkender, is quoted as saying: 'Blackler's job was to keep Harold spick and span, he was to remove the shine from Harold's face and the great bags from under his eyes which develop during the campaign and make a bad picture.' Falkender is open about their aim: 'We wanted to present a very competent, clear-cut, well-groomed image, which is what people expect of their leaders – frankly.'[12]

The current leader of the Labour party, Neil Kinnock, was elected partly because he was perceived to be 'good on television'. He was elected despite the fact that he had never served in government and despite the fact that he had less experience than the other contenders for the post. At the time he was thought to be good-looking; a long article on his appeal to lady voters even appeared in the *Sun*. However, Mr Kinnock does suffer from one of the problems that at least one American political consultant puts as a strong negative – he is bald. But, like Mrs Thatcher's, Mr Kinnock's hairstyle changed once he had won the leadership contest.

Previously he had favoured what Clive James calls the 'wrap around-baldy' style of cover-up, in which long strands of hair are stretched over the bald area – sometimes known in Britain as the 'Bobby Charlton' after the hairstyle affected by the former English footballer of that name. Mr Kinnock was ridiculed by the then *Observer* TV critic as appearing with his hair 'Charltoning' in the wind. But shortly after his election he adopted what Clive James calls the 'own-up' style of baldness, where the hair is no longer scraped over the bald area. The advantage is that, whilst the baldness is more apparent, there can be no more jokes about the increasingly desperate attempts to conceal it, and the candidate can appear in a gust of wind without one long strand disassociating itself from one side of his head and hanging limply down past his ear.

Peter Mandelson, Labour's much-lauded former Director of Communications, the man responsible for the party's change of image in the eighties, told me that he believes such details are trivial. He maintains that the average voter is sharp enough to delve behind the candidate's mere 'look'. And yet Mr Kinnock *has* changed in appearance since he became party leader, as did Mrs Thatcher. John Major may have said that the 'image' makers would not change him, but the fact is that Shaun Woodward, the Conservative's recent Director of Communications (who resigned in July 1992) admits that Major's voice now sounds more authoritative in Parliament. Since Major's voice was the one aspect of his presentation which American consultants told me on his election *they* would change, can it be coincidence that it has? Is it really the case, as Shaun Woodward might say, that it's just a question of Mr Major growing into his job? The truth is that politicians in Britain *are* concerned with their appearance on TV and they listen to the advice of the experts. After all, as Sir Tim Bell admits, 'You have to be pretty vain to want to be a politician in the first place', since 'an election campaign's quite a vanity-orientated experience. . . . You go on television and everybody recognizes you in the street. They all know who you are. You're as famous as Bob Monkhouse and that's quite an achievement.'

Perhaps it is no accident that Sir Tim, when asked, chose to quote an example of the influence of the politician's physical appearance not from Britain, where he has many powerful friends among politicians, but from a campaign he orchestrated in Chile in an attempt to get General Pinochet's candidate elected in the Presidential elections. The candidate was called Hernan Buchi, a man whom Bell describes in negative terms as 'tall and thin. He eats yoghurt and he jogs and he doesn't drive cars. He goes to work on a bike. He lives on his own. He hasn't got any children.' In addition the candidate was Swiss or 'Swiss-Chilean'. The candidate clearly did not measure up to South American 'macho' standards. So what was the solution? Bell explains: 'We got a picture of him wearing a poncho, looking like Clint Eastwood out of one of those fabulous movies, and wrote underneath it, "*Buchi es el hombre*", which means "Buchi's the man" – and just ran it. There he was, the wind was blowing him and he had this distant gazing look into the future – and he's never looked like this. He looked fabulous. He looked like a real film star . . . *"Buchi es el hombre"*. Just great. Got him to 48 per cent. We lost, but we got him to 48 per cent.'

Bell now accepts that the fundamental problem with his stunning poster campaign was that it went against the candidate's character. He had committed the cardinal propaganda sin of dissonance – in reality Buchi was boring and dull. As we saw with Robert Goodman's work for Malcolm Wallop, a 'little stretch' is acceptable, whereas, as Edward Kennedy found when his propagandists tried to paint him as a family man, an outright inversion of the truth is potentially disastrous. But the especially revealing side of this story is that here you have Britain's top political consultant – albeit not in American terms a 'professional' since he also works in product advertising – admitting that appearance *does* matter, and that he nearly got a dull candidate elected on the basis of how he looked in a poster. So even the man who says the importance of looks is 'crap' has been known to try and win an election on looks alone.

British politicians use props just as much as the Americans. The Liberal Jeremy Thorpe scored a hit when he decided to campaign by hovercraft in the 1974 General Election. Most candidates plan glamorous foreign trips close to election time to show off their diplomatic expertise. Mrs Thatcher's trip to Moscow in 1987 was the most successful example, and Mr Kinnock's to Washington in the same year the least – this was the visit during which Ronald Reagan reportedly greeted Denis Healey, former Labour Defence Secretary, with the words: 'Hello again, Mr Ambassador'. Prime Ministers, like Presidents, have a built-in advantage on such foreign trips since they are able to meet foreign leaders of substance and power, and be seen surrounded by honour guards and police escorts, riding in bullet-proof limousines.

British Prime Ministers are forbidden to make use of Number 10 as a partisan prop in their party political broadcasts – a restriction that no American President suffers from – but this does not prevent them allowing in the documentary makers when election time looms. There was a brief time in the mid-1980s when it seemed that everyone could have access to the Prime Minister; she appeared in Jenny Barraclough's film about the history of Number

10 as well as Ruth Jackson's film *The Englishwoman's Wardrobe* in which she revealed that she bought her underwear from Marks and Spencer's.

There is one further problem which the British propagandist faces in his pursuit of the leader myth. In Britain the risk of the 'free' media exposing dissonance is greater than that faced by politicians in America. In Britain there are ten national daily newspapers, as well as a tradition that the leaders of the main parties debate fiercely amongst themselves in Parliament and answer voters' questions directly on network television programmes. It is simply not possible to protect a Prime Minister in the same way that Michael Deaver managed to protect Ronald Reagan in the 1984 American Presidential election. Sir Tim Bell says: 'There's an enormous role for the media and for the press here, and if all you do on television is a bit of "feel and touch" the press would take your trousers off the next day.' The most important consequence which arises from this inability to protect the leader is that it is easier, in Britain, for a candidate who is unattractive to make up for this disadvantage in other ways – specifically by articulacy and political acumen. If, as is the case in America, the chief method of political discourse is the thirty-second ad, then the candidate's physical appearance becomes infinitely greater in importance, especially since, as we have seen, Cook and McHenry's work shows that first impressions are when looks matter most.

None of this means that the British propagandist does not strive to create the leader myth – merely that he must be more circumspect about how he does it. Don't forget that the highlight of the 1987 British election propaganda battle was film director Hugh Hudson's autobiographical party election broadcast about Neil Kinnock, in which the candidate and his wife were seen strolling romantically over the Welsh hills. It was so successful that it raised Kinnock seventeen points in popularity. And remember John Schlesinger's 'Major returns to his roots' party election broadcast was a key part of the Conservatives' strategy in 1992 (see page 91).

Propagandists on both sides of the Atlantic – indeed increasingly everywhere that TV has influence – have discovered that television is by its very nature a story-telling medium, and that the greatest election story is always going to be the story of the candidate himself.

Where will this television pursuit of the leader myth end? Michael

Deaver, President Reagan's communications adviser, believes he knows: 'It's not hard to picture a scenario not unlike the TV programme *Dating Game*, where three candidates give their qualifications, smile, and answer questions about how old they were when they were allowed to car date, and the studio audience presses a button to indicate their favourite.'[13]

Notes

1. Welch, David: *Propaganda and the German Cinema 1933–45*

2. Jamieson, Kathleen Hall: *Packaging the Presidency*

3. McGinniss, Joe: *The Selling of the President, 1968*

4. Noonan, Peggy: *What I Saw at the Revolution*

5. Interviewed in *TV and the President* produced by Ailes Communications

6. Spero, Robert: *The Duping of the American Voter*

7. Jamieson, Kathleen Hall: *Packaging the Presidency*

8. Interviewed in *The Washington Version* produced by Brian Lapping Associates for BBC TV and Discovery Channel

9. Ailes, Roger: *You Are the Message*

10. McGinniss, Joe: *The Selling of the President, 1968*

11. Fallon, Ivan: *The Brothers – The Rise and Rise of Saatchi and Saatchi*

12. Cockerell, Michael: *Live from Number 10*

13. Deaver, Michael K., with Micky Herskowitz: *Behind the Scenes*

Chapter Three

Themes Not Policies

Even in today's television age the candidate cannot talk only of himself, he must also talk of his political intentions. Since the medium of television militates against information-led propaganda, how to present political policy is one of the propagandist's most difficult problems. Fortunately for the aspiring propagandist, the master has been here before him.

Lessons from the master

Goebbels and the Nazis did not lack firm policies. They pointed out where the trouble with Germany lay – with the Jews, the plutocrats and a system of parliamentary democracy that had caused chaos. Hitler's *Mein Kampf* is not a book written in an effort to achieve a high 'like' quotient – it is a book brimming with statements of future intention.

How should these policies be communicated to the people? That was the task entrusted to Goebbels. To start with, he knew with passion how *not* to do it – he knew it would be counter-productive just to launch into a detailed recitation of exactly what the Nazis' policies were. Goebbels knew, twenty-five years before Tony Schwartz and his theory of 'partipulation', that film propaganda has to be a partnership between the propagandist and his audience. The propagandist must learn what the audience itself feels, and then try and link his propaganda to preconceived views: perhaps by shifting existing views a little, but never seeking in one swift blow to overturn them. To this end Goebbels hit on two related rules: messages must be capable of being simply understood and of bearing repetition. He wrote in his diary:

> Knowledgeable people hold that the oftener you treat a subject
> the more indifferent the public grows to it. That is not the case. It
> depends how the subject is handled. If one can contrive always to
> show it in a new light, always to pile up the evidence against it,
> and to bring fresh arguments to one's side to bear, public interest
> will never flag; on the contrary it will increase.

Wilfred Von Oven, Goebbels's own personal attaché for the last few years of the war, remembers how the Reichsminister explained the essence of propaganda to him: 'Propaganda is like a convoy in the war which has to make its way to the target under heavy military protection,' Goebbels told him. 'It has to adjust its marching speed to suit the slowest of the unit. That's how it is here. We have to do the same with our propaganda. All sophisticated propaganda is quite out of place. The masses don't understand irony. One has to concentrate quite simply on the basic message which one wants to achieve with the propaganda and one has to get it to the masses in the most popular and graphic manner possible.' Von Oven found these words difficult to reconcile with Goebbels's 'high intelligence and his education'. Von Oven was not the first Nazi to be astonished that an intellectual like Goebbels could aspire to such a wholly unintellectual approach.

Goebbels's genius rested to a degree on his ability to judge the speed of the 'convoy' and to think out 'fresh arguments' around the same theme. For example, he was determined to reinforce in the German people a sense of 'German-ness', to emphasize the qualities that made them as a people both different from and superior to others. This aim was partly achieved by showing newsreels of the victories of German sportspeople, the triumphs of German engineering and so on; but other less obvious ways of propagating the message included the making of an extraordinary feature film called *Ewiger Wald (The Eternal Forest)*, released in 1936. The film examines in lyrical terms the relationship of the German people with the forest – the forest symbolizing purity and simplicity. Accompanying literature started, 'No people can live without a forest. . . .' The film allows the audience itself to make the link that to be a German is to be a considerable person – a simple theme that was repeated again and again.

Where Goebbels actually had to change the public's perception, he trod warily. In promoting the Nazi policy on compulsory euthanasia, for instance, he ensured that the issue was dealt with in a sympathetic and sensitive way which allowed the audience to be gently led towards their own conclusion – a conclusion which, because of the skewed evidence laid before them, would be precisely the one Goebbels wanted. The film *Ich Klage An (I Accuse)*, released in 1941, was designed to put the case for euthanasia. The plot concerns a doctor who is eventually tried for the humanitarian killing of his desperately ill wife, who is shown begging her husband to release her from torment and pain. After the film was shown, discussion groups were held and the audience were led to form their 'own' conclusion that it was surely wrong that the poor doctor in the film was tried for a killing motivated by kindness. One might at first have thought that the man who supervised *Eternal Jew* would have made a film showing horror footage of mentally ill people, allied to a harsh commentary calling for their removal – but no.

A favourite method of promoting 'issues' was the use of the historical feature. A series of films like *Pour Le Mérite (For Merit)*, released in 1938, showed in historical terms how the settlement at the end of the First World War had been both disastrous and unfair on Germany. By involving the audience in the story of one individual character, films like this grabbed the attention of the audience and allowed them to extrapolate for themselves the broad propaganda conclusions that Goebbels wanted. A similar technique is used today on television consumer programmes, where an individual story is taken to represent a broader truth. One person is shown as, for example, the victim of an industrial accident. One personal story is dealt with in detail – the story of the victim's hospital visit, the court case – one person's despair and suffering. So the audience can identify with the plight of a single individual before being led to the general conclusion, drawn at the end of the item with a line like: 'And there are a hundred thousand cases like this – what should be done?' Goebbels would heartily approve of this technique of the visual presentation of ideas. He would have agreed with Stalin's notorious dictum, 'One death is a tragedy, a million is a statistic.'

This desire to tread carefully with public opinion – unless Goebbels knew that public opinion was predisposed to be sympathetic to his propaganda – clearly coloured his approach to telling 'The Big Lie' as instructed by *Mein Kampf*. Von Oven told me, 'I am being asked again and again if he lied all the time. Well, that's not true – though he did try to bend the truth to fit his ideas. He said to me very often when I came to him with difficult news, 'Look, you have to see it differently from what it says here. Instead you have to express it approximately this way,' and he always knew the right direction. 'But lying,' he kept saying to me, 'lying doesn't get us anywhere. One has to represent the truth in such a way that it becomes clear to the simplest of men with perhaps a correction here and a correction there. But, on the contrary,' he kept saying, 'straightforward lies, one day they come back and turn counter-productive.'

Under Goebbels the German newsreel aspired to be as consciously dramatic as possible in its presentation of issues, so it employed many more consciously filmic techniques than the equivalent Allied films did. To this end Goebbels issued a memo saying that German troops should always be photographed going from left to right; only enemies and 'sub-humans' should be seen going from right to left. (Since the eye moves most easily from left to right, any character in a film moving in this direction is followed more comfortably and the audience are thus potentially predisposed to like him.) The editing of Nazi newsreels is often complex. Close-ups are used to register emotion and are intercut with other action. Goebbels, as we have seen, strived to entertain with his propaganda, so a number of entertainment-based techniques can be seen in the newsreels – like the use of music to heighten emotional impact.

Goebbels felt it was vital to be cautious in putting any new issue forward – to move slowly, to create a simple message and then repeat it, ideally to engage the audience by relating his propaganda to their needs. These are just the techniques which American TV consultants use today.

The tyranny of the polls

Before the invention of film or television the candidate could easily judge voters' reactions to his manifesto. If they cheered him at public meetings they liked it; if they booed him they hated it. But once television took firm hold of the electoral process post-war American propagandists had no simple way of determining voters' responses to a particular issue. And so was born a brother to the democratic propagandist – the pollster.

It began simply enough, just by asking a sample group of voters what they thought of a particular issue or particular politician. Polling in itself was not a hindrance to the politician of conviction – it could be a help. But then, slowly, step by step, polling began to alter the way politicians acted; it began to dictate what they would say, not just how they would say it. Raymond Strother puts the consultant's case plainly enough: 'If a candidate feels strongly about fifteen different issues but only three of them are important to the public, you don't waste all of your time on the other twelve. You highlight those three. Well, people would say that's dishonest, but why spend money on issues that no one cares about but you and the candidate?'

Dottie Lynch, now Political Editor of CBS News, began work as a pollster in the 1970s. She detects a major shift not just in the influence of pollsters but in the effect of polls on candidates. When she started, she says, 'The assumption was that an incumbent would run on his record.' But then, by the mid-1980s, she began to discover 'more and more candidates who either didn't have records or didn't have positions fully formed on issues'. What the candidate began to do was to say: 'What do the polls tell me I ought to believe?' This is a logical, but philosophically radical, step from asking: 'What do the polls tell me about what the voters think of my beliefs?' The change is fundamental. It means that a politician need not really believe in anything and yet can still be successful – arguably more successful ·

than someone with committed beliefs, because such a politician is less flexible to 'voter response'. Dottie Lynch recalls a case where she asked a candidate for his position on abortion, probably one of the two or three absolutely fundamental questions of principle for the American politician; the candidate replied: 'Well, you know, I haven't seen the numbers yet.' If a candidate is prepared to alter his view on the legality of abortion on the basis of a poll, then it seems safe to conclude that he holds no policy on which he will not change his initial view (assuming he has an initial view to change). Lynch admits she found the actions of such 'new-wave' politicians 'distressing'.

Polling is becoming ever more sophisticated. Some pollsters actually use a laser-beam device, which is aimed at the retina of the human eye to spot which area of the TV screen is being looked at. Often such advanced techniques are used to find answers to what are (at first sight) trivial questions. We filmed one focus group in Detroit where a paid cross-section of voters were listening to tapes of prospective candidates' voices and then being asked questions like: 'Who sounds more decisive? What social class would you place this voice in? Does it sound strong or weak?' Few of the questions were related to the content of the actual statements – almost all were related to the style in which the words were spoken. The whole thrust of these pollsters' research was based on the premise that when issues are expressed on television presentation is more important than content.

The exact choice of who should be in a selected focus group is made with great care. It is not simply a question of discovering what an average cross-section of voters thinks. Voters who express support for the candidate are quizzed, as are voters who support his opponent – as are, most crucially of all, voters who are wavering. It was the results of a confidential focus group meeting in Paramus, New Jersey, of a group of voters who had voted for Reagan but were considering switching to Dukakis, that inspired the Bush attack in 1988 on the twin issues of the pledge of allegiance (Dukakis had vetoed Massachusetts legislation making it compulsory) and the prison furlough programme (during which a convicted murderer, Willie Horton, had been released for a weekend) (see page 105). It is significant that both these issues are minor alongside the monumental issues of state confronting any President – such as defence, foreign policy and the national debt. But major issues are hard to test in focus groups and even harder to express in TV terms. So it's issues which relate to individual stories and which generate emotion that are in demand – no matter how trivial.

This new sophistication in polling also means that the social composition of each particular voting district is carefully studied by the propagandist. In one consultant's office I saw two of the firm's partners poring over spreadsheets showing the exact breakdown of social class in each separate TV-served area. The plan was to show a different commercial in each district. In the ghetto it was a commercial calling for more employment opportunities for the inner cities; in the affluent middle-class suburbs it was a commercial calling for more resources for the police to help fight crime; and so on. So it isn't a question of having just *one* policy decided by the pollsters – the candidate might have several policies specially targeted to specific voters' needs.

A new technique in polling, identified by Dottie Lynch, involves connecting a current problem with a historical one. So a pollster might check how the voter feels about the measures that were taken against Hitler; assuming the data was favourable, the politician might then try to link in any current conflict to the historical one. For instance, if the statement 'Saddam Hussein is another Hitler' is repeated enough times, the politician hopes that the positive acceptance of the historical necessity of war against Hitler will spill over into the voter feeling the same about the necessity for war with Saddam Hussein.

The problem with polls

Some consultants actually say: 'What's the big concern about using polls in this way? It's ultimate democracy, isn't it?' So it is important to rehearse the arguments as to why such polling is dangerous to a democracy.

First, in answering polls the public is often responding to information which has been given on television. This means that on complex issues they are making their minds up on the basis of two- or three-minute news reports – that is, on insufficient information.

Second, the public's response to an issue may change daily and be wildly inconsistent. It is rumoured that a factor in George Bush's decision to end the Gulf War was a poll which showed that the American public wanted it to stop. So he stopped the war. A week later another poll showed that a substantial number of voters now believed that the war should have been continued until Saddam Hussein had been captured or disposed of. In such a situation a politician can hardly argue: 'You can't criticize me because I did what you wanted at the time.' One of the consequences of expediency is lack of consistency – you will never wake up in the morning and know what you believe until you read the polls. In the end, you may find yourself believing something today that is at odds with what you believed yesterday or will believe tomorrow.

Third, and most important, forming policy based essentially on polls negates leadership. You cannot be a leader and a follower at the same time, and if a politician follows the polls he is precisely that – a follower. It is not hard to think of great events in history that might have been very different if politicians had been led by polls. What if Winston Churchill had listened to pollsters during the 1930s and heeded their warnings that 'the British are really bored with you banging on about the dangers of German rearmament'? And what about Abraham Lincoln and the American Civil War? Peggy Noonan reveals what she thinks Lincoln would have done if he had received polls showing a majority against the war:

> One of the reasons Lincoln was great is that he would have looked at the data presented by his pollster and said something like, 'I see they're against the war, so I guess I'll have to communicate the argument for keeping the Union together better than I have.' He would not have said, 'Gee, they're against it – guess I better not spend my capital on a losing game just to help the Negroes!'[1]

But probably the finest rebuttal of the power of the polls was given by Dr Martin Luther King Jnr (an eloquent supporter of the anti-Vietnam War lobby) in a sermon he delivered on 31 March 1968 at the National Episcopal Cathedral in Washington:

> One day a newsman came to me and said, 'Dr King, don't you think you're going to have to stop, now, opposing the war and

move more in line with the administration's policy? As I
understand it, it has hurt the budget of your organization and
people who once respected you have lost respect for you. Don't
you feel that you've really got to change your position?' I looked at
him and I had to say, 'Sir, I'm sorry you don't know me. I'm not a
consensus leader. I do not determine what is right and wrong by
looking at the budget of the Southern Christian Leadership
Conference. I've not taken a sort of Gallup poll of the majority
opinion. Ultimately a genuine leader is not a searcher for
consensus, but a moulder of consensus.'[2]

Even consultants themselves are beginning to be concerned about
the lack of any conviction shown by many prospective candidates.
Experienced Southern consultant Jim Duffy says, 'It's consistently a
battle to try and get people into this business who really have a
clearly thought out political philosophy.' Duffy reveals that a 'lot' of
people come through his door who want to be Governors, Senators,
Congressmen and 'they sit down. They look great. You go through –
"Can you raise money?" "Yes." "Do you have a political base?" "Yes."
They answer all the right political questions and then you get down
to: "Well, what is it that you offer? Why should people vote for
you?" And you get these kind of looks like: "Uh? Well, that's your
job." And we kind of look at each other and go, "Oh, boy!"'

Duffy believes that unless the candidate actually generates some
policy opinions himself then 'there's no way we can sell him'. He
says: 'If there's one quality I look for, it's a candidate that actually
believes in something. Now if you believe in something then we can
poll it, we can test it, we can – even if it's radical – find ways to
present it in its best light. But if there's not some reason that drives
someone to run that's difficult.' Duffy asserts that even experienced
politicians in America 'are just petrified to stand up and say, "Let me
tell you what I believe. I believe X. I believe Y. I believe Z. And if
you don't believe X, Y and Z then you ought to vote for somebody
else because you'll waste your vote on me."'

Duffy's views are radical. They certainly don't fit into the pattern
of most consultants' philosophy. The common view is best
expressed in the words of Roger Ailes, the most successful political
consultant of recent years. 'Above all,' he says, 'never discuss the

hard realities of governance – that's suicide.'[3] Ailes is absolutely clear that the realities of TV campaigning mean it is not just futile for a candidate to discuss issues in his propaganda – it is positively dangerous as well. 'If we came out with a sweeping view of how to change things,' says Ailes, 'there are going to be some flaws in it. And the next thirty days of stories are going to be about the flaws. Therefore, you have made a terrible mistake in trying to present an idea which may be helpful.'

Relating issues to themes

However, not even Roger Ailes thinks that the candidate should say *nothing* about his future political programme. So the solution most favoured by TV consultants is to instruct their candidates to speak not about issues but about themes. One of the first ever Presidential adverts, *Eisenhower Talks to the Nation*, used this technique brilliantly. Answering a stooge voter's question about specific problem issues, Eisenhower replied firmly, 'We're going to put an end to these national scandals.' What a clever response. How can such a promise to 'put an end to these national scandals' ever be tested? Who decides when a scandal is at an end? Yet as a TV answer it sounds perfectly plausible.

Professor Kathleen Jamieson points out a crucial change in the way Ronald Reagan presented his foreign policy views which perfectly illustrates the difference between stating the issue and stating the theme. In 1976 he stated his position on the future of the Panama Canal with the catchy slogan: 'We built it and we're going to keep it.' No shilly-shallying around trying to guess the man's true policy there. But in a Presidential advert in 1980 he stated his view that a strong defence was important for America by saying: 'Our foreign policy has been based on the fear of not being liked. Well, it's nice to be liked. But it's more important to be respected.' Very clever. The illusion of substance is created, but there can be no come-back from the voter. Reagan and his advisers must have realized that it was both foolish and unnecessary to itemize just what they would do to achieve the goal of being 'respected'. How much would they raise the defence budget? Where would they get the money from? No, better stick to the fine-sounding 'theme' of making America 'respected'.[4]

With Ailes as an adviser you would think that George Bush would have learnt the lesson of never stating direct policy intentions during an election – but he didn't. By far his biggest communications mistake in the 1988 election campaign was to utter the fateful words: 'Read my lips: no new taxes.' It meant that when he subsequently raised taxes there was no alternative but to appear to have broken his promise. How he must have wished he'd talked about the underlying theme instead, and said something like: 'I'm committed totally to a system of fair taxation and I promise that taxation will never become an unjust burden.' If he subsequently had to raise taxes – well, who is to say what is just or unjust?

It is television which has enabled the politician to speak in such a way. American television with its commercial pressures is the ideal medium for the politician who talks in entertainment-orientated themes, like Reagan's vision of the 'city on the hill', and who relies on the polls for guidance on specific issues. The one word that I heard used to describe such a political philosophy was 'fluid'. One leading consultant told me of his candidate, 'Boy, you won't believe just how fluid our guy can be. Don't you just love him?' Do we? And if we don't, shouldn't we apportion some of the blame to television itself? Professor Postman states unequivocally, 'You cannot do political philosophy on television. Its form works against the content.' And 'Under the governance of the printing press, discourse in America was different from what it is now – generally coherent, serious and rational; under the governance of television, it has become shrivelled and absurd.'[5] Whether or not you agree that political discourse has become 'shrivelled and absurd', it is clear that it is television which has enabled the propagandist to put the candidate's case without recourse to specific promises on issues. For the politician who lacks conviction but has charming personal habits and appearance there has never been a better time to seek office.

Recent British themes

The British General Election of April 1992 saw both the Labour and the Conservative parties seek American advice on polling. Though all of the individuals involved refuse to comment – surely they can't think it would be embarrassing for British voters to learn that Americans were involved in their election – it seems certain that the Conservatives sought the advice of the Republican pollster Richard Wirthlin and the Labour party employed the Democratic consultants Doak and Schrum. It is therefore fittingly ironic that the 1992 election will go down in history as a contest the pollsters got wrong. No one predicted the actual result, a clear Conservative win.

For the Conservatives, Shaun Woodward had always known that his greatest asset was John Major. The whole thematic idea of the 'classless' society could in fact be a synonym for Major's own character and achievement. So it was no accident that the very first Tory party election broadcast was John Schlesinger's film of John Major's journey back to his roots in Brixton. The film's only error was to concentrate on shots of John Major talking about his early life from the back of a comfortable car – the visual image projected was hardly that of an accessible man of the people.

The significance of this broadcast was immense. Not for what it actually said, which was very little, but for the fact that it demonstrated the message the Conservatives wanted to get over to the people at the very start of the campaign: John Major is a nice man. Not John Major is a fine Prime Minister and here are his policies. Simply John Major is the sort of person you'd like to spend time with. This is a new kind of political communication, a kind that could only have been enthusiastically promoted by someone who has worked in television, who knows that television propaganda deals best with people and not with policies.

The clue that the Schlesinger film of John Major gave to the Conservatives' election strategy was that their chief election theme *was* John Major. Not John Major's team or John Major's policies but John Major the man. To this end Woodward had always planned that the presentation of John Major should be very different from the way Mrs Thatcher has been presented. Out went the big set piece rallies, in came the conversational 'chats' – John Major sitting on a high stool surrounded by a carefully selected audience of sympathizers. At least one critic compared this style of presentation with Val Doonican's light entertainment TV show. A more accurate comparison would have been film of George Bush's 'Friendly Chats' during his 1988 Presidential campaign, in the course of which Bush also sat on a high stool surrounded by a sympathetic audience. This format was almost certainly the model for the Tory version.

Later in the campaign, the stool was changed in favour of a stand up lectern against a backdrop of deepest blue, though once more Major spoke only to a committed audience of Conservatives. It is easy to understand the logic behind this form of presentation since it was one in which Major could perform in a controlled environment. However, as a persuasive technique it simply didn't appear to work.

As the Tories appeared to be making no advance in the polls the critics turned on Shaun Woodward and his youthful team at Central Office. Trevor Fishlock, writing in the *Sunday Telegraph* on 29 March, said that 'On the Tory trail the blood ran like glue,' and further, 'part of the problem may be that many of Major's team are dashing young subalterns who think they know everything; what are needed here are a few battered old sergeants who know something.'

It would be inaccurate to describe the Prime Minister as a 'battered old sergeant' but it was John Major himself who was to invent the perfect way he should be presented: the soap box. Major first stood on his soap box in Luton on 28 March, shouting out to a crowd of bemused Saturday shoppers the reasons why they should vote Tory. The image made wonderful television. Here was a Prime Minister who was exposing himself to the barracking of the ordinary voter, who was dodging (sometimes not dodging) the occasional egg, who was prepared to come out of his controlled and packaged TV set. As Frank Johnson saw it: 'Now he [Major] was really human – unscripted, jokey, even a bit passionate.'

Worries were expressed that the soap box made Major look more like the challenger than the incumbent. But this was precisely the technique's advantage. For whilst John Major was perceived as out on his soap box speaking to the people in the shopping centres of suburban Britain, the leader of the opposition was participating in one of the most misjudged campaign presentational events of recent political history – the Labour party rally in Sheffield. The Sheffield rally could have been a carbon copy of the sort of presidential rallies of which Mrs Thatcher was so fond. Ten thousand adoring fans cheered Neil and Glenys Kinnock's arrival into the arena (after they had watched on a giant video screen their landing by helicopter). Neil Kinnock was introduced as 'the next Prime Minister' and he waved and gestured enthusiastically at the screaming crowd. Harvey Thomas, who had organized many similar extravaganzas for the Conservatives, and who had ceased his involvement with Central Office after the arrival of Shaun Woodward, said on BBC radio how impressed he was with the Labour rally. But impressive though the spectacle might have been, it sent all the wrong messages to the viewer watching on television. The contrast with that nice Mr Major could not have been greater. Here was Neil Kinnock almost holding a victory rally for an election that had not yet been won and there was Mr Major, out in the wet and cold, with no more of a presentational tool than his soap box, doing his best to solicit his votes individually.

Labour's image problem was exacerbated by the fact that whilst the Conservatives had deliberately made John Major the centre piece of their campaign, the Labour Party communications team had apparently felt compelled to protect Neil Kinnock from the hostile tabloid press. Neil Kinnock was most definitely not the Labour party's central theme. It was the National Health Service that was always going to be the big Labour issue. The method by which they mounted their attack on the Conservatives is dealt with in the next chapter.

Notes

1. Noonan, Peggy: *What I saw at the Revolution*

2. King, Martin Luther Jnr: *A Testament of Hope*

3. From a seminar at the Barone Center for Press, Politics and Public Policy, John F. Kennedy School of Government, Harvard University

4. Jamieson, Kathleen Hall: *Packaging the Presidency*

5. Postman, Neil: *Amusing Ourselves to Death*

Chapter Four

Dealing with the Enemy

The wise propagandist knows that an enemy is his most important asset. A clearly defined enemy brings many benefits. Attacking the enemy makes your candidate look strong while giving away nothing about his own policy which could make him vulnerable to attack himself. An enemy provides focus for the candidate's followers; they can define themselves by identifying the enemy they collectively dislike – a task that is easier than laboriously deciding what exactly is their own common ground. An enemy allows the candidate to ascribe blame for the nation's ills in a safe yet apparently challenging way. Enemies are so important to today's propagandists that if they do not exist they have to be invented.

Lessons from the master

Goebbels relished his enemies, but he knew that the most important rule in selecting them was to make sure that the population was already predisposed to dislike them. In *Harper's* magazine in 1936 Aldous Huxley produced some of the wisest words ever written on the subject: 'Propaganda gives force and direction to the successive movements of popular feeling and desire; but it does not do much to create these movements. The propagandist is a man who canalizes an already existing stream. In a land where there is no water he digs in vain.' Goebbels's own propaganda against his enemies worked best when he 'canalized the existing stream'. When he attempted to work where there was no predisposition, he failed.

In the late 1920s when Goebbels arrived in Berlin there were only about five hundred active members of the Nazi party. He knew he had to create drama. So he turned up with his small but loyal following and caused disorder at meetings of the Nazis' most politically acceptable enemy, the Communists. In one riot at the Pharus assembly rooms nearly a hundred people were hurt – the next day three thousand new members joined the Nazi party. Goebbels almost encouraged the Communists to fight back, knowing that the tougher the perceived enemy the more the Nazis would benefit. After all, as one modern consultant told me, 'You don't send Superman against a shoplifter, you send him against King Kong.'

Goebbels luxuriated in attack. The Communist papers nicknamed him the 'super-gangster', so he signed his articles 'J.G. Oberbandit' (J.G. Super-Gangster).[1] He was always true to his philosophy: 'Attack before the adversary has had any chance to get in his blow and confine him to defensive tactics and fight him till he's done!'

After the Nazis came to power in 1933 the Communists were banned and became an ineffective enemy within Germany's borders. But the Jews remained. They could be seen everywhere, in shops, on the streets – and many of them were rich. In almost every way the Jews were the perfect enemy. They were a traditional scapegoat – even Shakespeare had written arguably anti-Semitic propaganda in *The Merchant of Venice*. Goebbels sought to capitalize on this common prejudice and make Jew-hating acceptable to the German population as a whole. Here was a stream of historical belief that only needed a little 'canalization' to prove devastating.

Goebbels himself seems to have had little personal animosity towards Jewish culture, which makes his subsequent behaviour all the more chilling. He was actually an admirer of Jewish literature and talent and would shout to his staff: 'What I need are a couple of clever Jews to help me!'

Although Goebbels called for a boycott of all Jewish businesses as early as March 1933, it was not until the end of the thirties that he authorized the production of anti-Jewish feature films. It was as if

Goebbels knew the force, once unleashed, that a dramatic *film-led* propaganda attack on the Jews would have on both national and world opinion. It was only after the Second World War had begun that wide-reaching and powerful anti-Semitic attacks were made on film. And these attempted to provide implicit justification for the transportation of Jews to the east.

The failure of *The Eternal Jew*, directed by Fritz Hippler, has already been discussed. Even given the predisposition of the German population to dislike the Jews, the sight of rats personifying Jews was clearly extreme. More successful was *Jud Süss* ('*Jew Süss*'), another anti-Jewish film based on a distortion of a novel by Lion Feuchtwanger, which dealt with the alleged machinations of the Jewish race and the historical ability of one of its members, Jew Süss, to weasel his way into the Gentile world of eighteenth-century Württemberg. In one particularly unpleasant scene a perfect specimen of Aryan womanhood (played by Christine Soderbaum) is raped by Jew Süss whilst her husband is tortured nearby. Because the film employs one of Goebbels's favourite film propaganda techniques – the historical representing the present – it is a disturbingly effective piece of propaganda. At one level it is a simple but strong dramatic tale. It is the audience who make the assumption that the horrific actions of the individual Jew Süss are representative of the immorality of the entire Jewish race.

Although Goebbels often hired women because he was attracted to them, he was not attracted to Christine Soderbaum, the actress he ordered to play Dorothea in *Jud Süss*. But he realized that, since she had the fair hair, blue eyes and clear skin of the archetypical Aryan, the sight of her being raped by a Jew would be all the more horrific. She recalls that the Propaganda Ministry issued a command implying that those who had been ordered to appear in *Jud Süss* had better comply and 'Those who refuse to carry out orders – well: Adios. And that was of course a frightening shock.' Soderbaum added: 'If I hadn't done it, then someone else would. I didn't act in it alone.' She wants the world to remember that when films like this were being made the reality of what was actually happening to the Jews was unknown. 'One sees it today differently,' she says. 'Today we have seen terrible pictures of the concentration camps. Then it becomes much worse suddenly and one says: "For Heaven's sake! I helped with this?"'

LEFT: The great persuader – Dr Josef Goebbels, Reichsminister of Propaganda, on his 45th birthday, 1942

BELOW: Goebbels and Hitler at a Gigli concert, 1933. Goebbels's wife, Magda, is on the far left

LEFT: Tony Schwartz's notorious *Little Girl and the Daisy* ad. The images were so powerful that the ad was only shown once during the 1964 Presidential campaign

VOTE FOR PRESIDENT JOHNSON ON NOVEMBER 3.

RIGHT TOP: Michael Deaver with his most famous client, Ronald Reagan

RIGHT: Roger Ailes briefing Bush's campaign staff on his TV image

ABOVE: 'Shooting from the hip' – Reagan the film star becomes president

LEFT: Reagan stumbles on the steps of Air Force One – the one slip-up in Michael Deaver's 1984 Presidential campaign

RIGHT TOP: The wrong image – Mrs Thatcher in a tank reinforced voters' perception of her as 'gung-ho'

RIGHT: The right image – Harold Macmillan's astrakhan hat symbolized the friendship he wished to establish with the Russians in 1959

LEFT: The unelectable president? Would Abraham Lincoln create problems for the image-makers today?

BELOW LEFT: It's not real unless it's on TV – even if you're there. Vice-President George Bush's acceptance speech, August 1984

OPPOSITE TOP LEFT and OPPOSITE TOP RIGHT: Kinnock the young MP and later party leader. Out went the Bobby Charlton hairstyle and tweed jacket, in came the glasses and blue suit

RIGHT: The poster that broke Labour in the 1992 General Election

ATIONAL SOLUS

STROUTS PLACE E2

LABOUR'S TAX BOMBSHELL.

YOU'D PAY £1,250 MORE TAX A YEAR UNDER LABOUR.

Labour's Manifesto promises would cost the average tax-payer an extra £1,250 a year

CONSERVATIVE

TOP and LEFT: The 1992 election – Labour's presidential-style Sheffield rally proved a stark contrast to Major's soap box – the prize-winning image of the Tory campaign

How can one quantify the impact on the German population of works like *Jud Süss*? Did such films really play a significant part in the committing of war crimes? The Nuremberg War Trials failed to answer such questions adequately – questions which still trouble psychologists today as they ponder the effect of 'video nasties'. Many of those involved in films like *Jud Süss* say that the effect is minimal, that dramatic works are just that – works of drama and imagination. But one significant fact about *Jud Süss* should be remembered: Himmler thought the film so effective that he issued an order that every SS man must see it, including the guards at Auschwitz.

Goebbels's anti-Jewish propaganda worked because it was focused. His propaganda against the British, on the other hand, shows exactly what happens when you do not wholeheartedly 'canalize an existing stream'. His major problem with his anti-British propaganda was that he himself had more than a sneaking admiration for the British and their lifestyle. Wilfred Von Oven remembers that Goebbels was 'immensely enthusiastic about England and the English leadership and, when talking about his house at Lanke (which was in the middle of a forest), he kept saying that, though he himself was a "town" person, life in the country was important because the English leadership grew up in the country'.

An early Nazi press directive said: 'Do not attack the English people, but the leading individuals in British society who have guided England into the encirclement policy. Attack particularly the Jews, international capitalism, and the fiancial interests.' The early Nazi feature films, like *Ein Mann Will Nach Deutschland (A Man Must Return to Germany)*, released in 1934, even went so far as to show the British *en masse* as a worthy enemy to be respected. Indeed, between 1936 and 1939 there was not one anti-British feature film made.

In the early years of the war there were a series of clumsy filmic attacks on the British. *Gentlemen* attempted to expose the hypocrisy of the English class system. *Die Englische Krankheit (The English Sickness)* revealed how the Nazis believed that the British had deliberately encouraged the spread of rickets in Germany during the First World War. Goebbels even made a disaster movie based on the sinking of the *Titanic*. The Germans tried to show that the ship sank because the aristocratic British officers were so incompetent that they hit the iceberg. This film failed completely: since the audience knew the fate of the *Titanic* beforehand, they were predisposed to be sympathetic to the victims on board and so missed the propaganda point.

Die Rothschilds Aktien von Waterloo (The Rothschilds' Shares in Waterloo), released in 1940, illustrated how the Jewish bankers the Rothschilds gained their wealth by exploitation, and also how it was in fact the British who won the battle of Waterloo – it was the Prussians who deserved all the credit. 'Lord' Wellington (as the film called him) is depicted as a foolish pleasure-seeker. The film is a perfect example of how *not* to create propaganda against an enemy. There is no single enemy on whom to focus; the attacks are too diverse and confused. Hitler himself wrote in *Mein Kampf* about the importance of simplicity in this area of propaganda: 'The leader of genius must have the ability to make different opponents appear as if they belonged to one category.' As Fritz Hippler said of *The Rothschilds' Shares in Waterloo*, the audience must know 'whom should I love and whom should I hate'. The film is a morass of anti-Jewish and anti-British propaganda, with the central problem of lack of conviction behind the hatred of the British. It is a classic example of the truth of Huxley's belief that the propagandist must 'canalize an existing stream'. The plain fact was that many Nazis admired the British; they didn't want to fight them, and their propaganda implicitly reflected this.

Goebbels was far from his best in his attacks on the British, but it was one of the few areas in which he failed. Many modern propagandists, on the other hand, make the same mistake throughout their work. A colleague of mine, whilst filming in Iran at the time of Khomeini, saw the following slogan painted in English on a wall: 'THE ISRAELIS ARE WORSE THAN THE AMERICANS. THE AMERICANS ARE WORSE THAN THE BRITISH. THE BRITISH ARE WORSE THAN THE ISRAELIS – THEY ARE EACH WORSE THAN EACH OTHER!' That is a textbook example of how not to attack an enemy.

The master in defeat

But what if the enemy seems to be gaining the upper hand? All the propaganda in the world couldn't deceive the Germans into thinking that after the debacle of Stalingrad they were actually winning. It was at just this time that Goebbels revealed his true mastery of propaganda.

He dealt with the prospect of defeat by the enemy in three ways. First, he told the Germans of the barbarism of the Communists – how rape and torture were inevitable, so that there was no possibility of giving up. Second, he called for defiance and exhorted the population to make a commitment to 'total war' (as in his famous speech in February 1943) – war at whatever cost. Third, and most important, he set out to entertain and inspire, calling on the people to hold out just long enough for the completion of the 'secret weapon' which he had promised would materialize to save them.

The story of the making of the film *Kolberg* perfectly illustrates Goebbels's approach to defeat. This dramatic historical picture was completed only weeks before the end of the war. The action concerned the siege of Kolberg in East Prussia in 1806–7 during the Napoleonic Wars. History was conveniently rewritten to show how the Germans rebuffed fierce French attacks and held the town; in fact Kolberg had eventually fallen to the French. The film is packed with historical messages of defiance and heroism which the audience were meant to take as instructions on how they should live in the last days of the war. Implicit in the film is the belief that even if you die as an individual, the ideals of the Germany for which you are dying can never perish – not as long as you die heroically. The individual is unimportant except as a part of the whole German *Volk*.

Kolberg was a huge enterprise. It was shot in colour and involved the use of thousands of extras – over 100,000 troops were diverted from the front line to act in the film. Goebbels's aide, Von Oven, recalls that 'it was more important that the extras in his film were able to play roles which they could no longer play on the front as simple soldiers, because it no longer brought results'. Goebbels was playing the longest propaganda game of all – he was playing for the history books. Von Oven recalls, 'He set a lot of hope in *Kolberg*,' praying that it would so inspire the Germans that they would carry on just long enough for the 'unnatural alliance' between western capitalism and Soviet Marxism to collapse.

Norbert Schultze, the German composer most famous for composing 'Lilli Marlene', was instructed to write the rousing and inspiring music for *Kolberg*. Schultze is frank in his assessment of the events surrounding the making of the film. 'It was madness what happened there, because the war was lost. Goebbels must have known this.' He knew that Goebbels was 'enthusiastic about the performance of the artists in such a film because he said: "it will survive us – the film *Kolberg* will survive us."'

Nothing shows more the extent to which Goebbels believed in the power of film propaganda than the words: 'It will survive us – the film *Kolberg* will survive us.' He knew that film was the only form of dramatic self-expression that could move masses as yet unborn. In a dramatic and self-revealing speech to his staff in the Propaganda Ministry, made after they had all seen *Kolberg* on 17 April 1945, he told them that there would be an even more splendid film shown in a hundred years' time and asked: 'Gentlemen, don't you want to play a part in this film, to be brought back to life in a hundred years' time? Everybody now has the chance to choose the part which he will play in a film a hundred years hence. I can assure you that it will be a fine and elevating picture. And for the sake of this prospect it is worth standing fast. Hold out now, so that a hundred years hence the audience does not hoot and whistle when you appear on the screen.'

In those last few weeks we can only speculate as to Goebbels's mental state. Certainly he appeared to stand up to the imminence of defeat much better than any of the other Reich leaders. There are newsreels of him in those final days travelling around bombed Berlin exhorting the citizens to greater effort. But the clue as to why he was actually doing this when all was lost lies in this speech to his staff. He was imagining an actor playing a part based on his own life story 'a hundred years hence'. If one imagines that Goebbels had long taken leave of the *reality* of his own life, then at last the horrific nature of his own end becomes lit by a glimmer of understanding. Why did Goebbels poison his own children and then watch as Magda, his wife, poisoned herself? Why did he shoot himself? Why did he not do what many other senior Nazis chose to do and try to save himself and his family? Was it because, in the words of Hans Otto Meissner, a German soldier who knew Goebbels, 'He believed in himself and he believed that he would continue his life in history. He thought it would be much better if his end would be to disappear, to kill himself. . . . It's a film ending, isn't it?' Exactly.

Goebbels must have hoped that one day he would be portrayed in an entertainment film which dramatized those last days, so he lived out his life as if he was dictating a film script. Unfortuntately for Goebbels and his cinematic plans, the murder of his children seems now not the heroic gesture of loyalty to the Führer he intended, but a callous and brutal stunt typical only of the amoral creature he had always been. But then, he did not live to turn his own actions into propaganda.

Fighting the enemy today

How Goebbels would have appreciated television's power to mount an attack! No longer would he have had to concentrate on moving the emotions for ninety or a hundred minutes, a timespan that makes it necessary to develop plot lines and characters. No, had he been practising his art in America during the last thirty years, he need only have tried to fill thirty seconds – a much easier task, since the shorter the timespan the easier it is to appear stronger as a candidate by saying something negative about your opponent rather than by saying something positive about yourself. As the veteran Republican consultant Robert Goodman says, 'It's more newsworthy when one candidate calls the other a son of a bitch than when he puts out his white paper on education.'[2]

The phenomenon of the eighties in American propaganda has been the rise of negativity in campaigning – especially in campaign adverts. Senator John Danforth calls it 'a national disgrace'. The *Washington Post* said of the 1988 Presidential campaign:

> It was not just a domestic disappointment but a national
> embarrassment . . . a screamingly tiresome, trivial, point-missing
> contest between two candidates who don't seem to be running for
> president so much as they seem to be having one of those
> headache-making fights that children are so good at staging in the
> back of the car when everyone's nerves are pretty much gone
> anyway.

However, it's vital to remember that it is the medium of television itself which has permitted such negativity. If an attack of any length is made on a politician in print, then that attack must be developed into a coherent argument – or it becomes nonsense. Any attempt to generate emotion by negative means through print without the mention of strong, concrete reasons why the opponent should not be elected inevitably looks inane. Goebbels seldom simply attacked the Jews as a 'concept' in any of his speeches; he gave mostly coherent (though inaccurate and unpleasant) reasons why the Jews should be oppressed. None of that would be necessary today. Goebbels could have used the rats-intercut-with-Jews scene from *The Eternal Jew* as a thirty-second advert – an advert which would stand a much greater chance of success than the same shots did when cut into a lengthy film. Such an ad would be a fine piece of emotional attack, unanswerable and unquestionable in rational terms. What is the political argument behind intercutting rats and Jews? That the Jews live like rats? If such a thing were to be alleged in print it would be unsustainable. But show such images on film and they become an appeal to the emotions which bypasses all intellectual judgement.

Tony Schwartz, another man who believes that TV propaganda works best on the emotions, has created some of the most memorable negative adverts (or 'attack' ads, as some consultants euphemistically call them) in recent years. A classic Schwartz negative ad, showing his acute perception of the strength of television as a means of attacking the enemy in a political contest, was one he made for the Hubert Humphrey campaign in 1968. It is stunningly simple. The camera starts on a close-up of the top right-hand side of a television set, and gradually the shot pulls out to reveal a caption on the TV screen: 'Spiro Agnew for Vice-President'. Heard throughout the ad is the sound of uncontrollable laughter. At the end of the ad another caption appears: 'This would be funny if it wasn't serious.' This advert is more revealing about the effectiveness of television as a thirty-second medium of negative propaganda than any other. It is extremely amusing. But what does it tell us about Spiro Agnew's fitness for office? What reasons does it give us not to vote for him? And how can Agnew possibly respond to such simple ridicule?

Schwartz defends the propriety of his ad by saying, 'We all felt that having this man for Vice-President was ridiculous and evoked laughter on the part of many people – or that they would see it as ridiculous if they heard the laughter.' It was a classic application of Schwartz's 'partipulation' theory – plug into something the voter already thinks – and therefore follow directly in the footsteps of Aldous Huxley and Josef Goebbels, who had both discovered some thirty years previously that the propagandist can only canalize an 'existing stream'.

Some of Schwartz's most powerful ads have never been aired on television, for though he makes them, control over whether they are shown is in the hands of the candidate and the overall campaign manager. One of these that he is most proud of was made for the McGovern campaign in 1972 – and never shown. He had been asked to make some spots that attacked Nixon's record, and the inspiration for this particular ad came from his young son. Schwartz was watching some news footage of a Vietnamese boy and his mother, both burnt by napalm. Schwartz's five-year-old son walked into the room, saw the pictures and remarked, 'Does the President know that planes bomb children?' Schwartz was stunned and inspired by the simplicity of his son's approach. The ad Schwartz subsequently made showed the same news footage of the woman, whilst towards the end of the thirty-second spot is heard the voice of Schwartz's son, saying exactly what he had spontaneously exclaimed to his father on first seeing the footage: 'Does the President know that planes bomb children?'

The McGovern campaign team decided that this ad should not appear. Perhaps they felt it was too strong. Maybe they decided it was unfair – because it is, of course, monumentally unfair. It represents precisely the logic and understanding that a five-year-old would bring to the subject of the war in Vietnam. We have already seen how Joe Slade-White was hired for a multi-million dollar campaign on the judgement of an eight-year-old. Now here is an example of a Presidential advert designed by a five-year-old – because only a five-year-old would pose the simplistic question: 'Does the President know that planes bomb children?' An educated adult, hearing such a question, would respond: 'Are you really saying the President authorizes the bombing of civilians with napalm? That the President is personally reckless about where the bombs fall?' But that is the amoral beauty of ads like this. In thirty seconds the impression of a callous President is created – an impression almost impossible to refute.

The fundamental reason why this ad is discreditable is that it omits

103

to place the news footage in any context. How many civilians have been napalmed? Why did it happen? What is the Air Force doing about it? I put it to Tony Schwartz that the ad in no way dealt with the central point – should the Americans be in Vietnam or not – and that it omitted the crucial fact that in every war in history, including wars which were considered just and necessary, there have been tragic accidents where children have been killed. So this footage was in no way special to Vietnam. He replied simply that 'this symbolized a lot of people's feelings about the war'. So the justification for the creation of this ad was that it would 'plug into' people's disatisfaction – and incidentally lower the debate about the war to a level where five-year-olds could participate.

The Prince of Negativity

Schwartz, however, is not the most renowned 'attack' consultant. It is the Republican Roger Ailes who has been described as the 'Prince of Negativity'. Such was the vilification heaped on him after the 1988 election that in some subsequent elections the question of whether or not Ailes was employed by a Republican candidate became an issue for his Democratic opponent. In 1990 Senator Paul Simon said: 'As far as I'm concerned I'm running against Roger Ailes as much as Lyn Martin [his Republican opponent].' Early in 1990 Ailes complained that there was a 'nationally orchestrated campaign to take me out'. Perhaps it is no coincidence that Ailes's company no longer has his name in its title and is now known innocuously as the Media Team, and its public face is that of its new President, an energetic and fresh-faced consultant called Greg Stevens, rather than the bullish figure of Roger Ailes. Surprisingly for a man who is a media expert, Ailes blames the media for his reputation: 'The media are lazy, and instead of talking about the issues they'd rather talk about negative ads. The goddam newspaper is negative. Television is negative. That's the reality of life. The fascination in the media with the negative is universal.' Greg Stevens, Ailes's loyal lieutenant, is also a believer in the conspiracy theory behind the media attacks on Ailes and his associates. He puts it down to a press that is biased towards the Democratic party and says, 'They think it's OK for the Democrats to be aggressive and hit back hard. But Republicans have set this standard that they're a little bit above it. They're a little more refined. They come from the country club. They come from corporate America. So there's a belief that Republicans, in terms of running campaigns, are a little shy about some of these things. Well, we've turned that on its head and time after time, when a candidate is in trouble or a candidate is behind and needs to win, they end up calling on us because we have the track record of coming from behind and being just as aggressive as some of our friends on the Democratic side.' But bear in mind that it is not universally accepted that the Republicans have been the 'nice guys' of recent Presidential campaigns. After all, there was a twice-elected Republican President called Richard Nixon whose campaign managers were not famous for either their reticence or their ethics.

Stevens, not surprisingly, robustly defends Ailes's work during the 1988 election: 'There was this feeling that the Bush campaign which we produced for the media was harsh and aggressive in its advertising. Well, we have evidence that the Dukakis campaign produced nineteen ads attacking George Bush. We produced essentially three or four ads that attacked Michael Dukakis. We can't help it if our ads are more effective and memorable than their ads – which is the truth.'

The reason Greg Stevens sounds defensive, if not downright disingenuous, is because of one ad – probably the most famous negative ad since *The Little Girl and the Daisy*. It came to be known as the Willie Horton ad, but is referred to by Ailes's team as the furlough ad, and it deals with a penal policy operated by Michael Dukakis as Governor of Massachusetts. It owes its origins to the ubiquitous forerunner of all modern TV propaganda – the focus group. The late Lee Atwater, Chairman of the Republican National Committee, had examined the data from a focus group which contained a classic cross-section of 'floating' Democratic voters. These guinea pigs were tested to find the particular points of Dukakis's record that they were most concerned about. Out of this focus group came two issues of importance – Dukakis's decision not to make the reciting of the pledge of allegiance compulsory in schools, and the furlough release programme which his state had operated. As part of this programme convicted prisoners were allowed home on weekend passes as they neared the end of their sentence. Atwater was excited. The former issue could be used to 'partipulate' the voter into remembering that Dukakis was of 'foreign' origin and therefore by implication the institutions of America were not safe in his hands; and the latter issue could be used to illustrate the one concept that almost all Republican consultants turn to in their negative campaigning – that their Democratic opponent is 'soft on crime'.

In the case of the furlough issue there was a memorable story to back the ad up – the fact that at least one convict released under the system, a black man called Willie Horton, had committed acts of murder and rape whilst out on furlough. Atwater realized the potent terror that such a story would cause in middle-class America. A black man is released, only to rape and murder again – a classic tale of the consequences of liberalism. Except, of course, for the fact that the story told in such terms is dishonest: the furlough programme had actually been originated in Massachusetts by Frank Sargent, a Republican Governor, and at least forty-five other states had a similar system of weekend release. These facts were lost, because the image of a 'liberal' Governor setting free convicted felons to murder and rape fitted precisely into most voters' preconceived stereotype – particularly when the felon concerned was black.

The ad that Ailes and his team made on the furlough theme has unusually high 'production values': that is to say, it is clear that both time and money were spent on it. The ad shows a line of men in prison garb walking towards a revolving door set into the prison perimeter bars. No sooner have they reached the door than they spin round and start walking back to camera again. The whole picture has a deep and troubling red tint to it, and there is a staggered zoom in to the prisoners to give a sense of tension and aggression. The commentary voice is that of a thousand Clint Eastwood trailers – that specially deep, gravelly voice that tells of future thrilling attractions. Only in this case the voice is warning us of terrible past decisions. 'Governor Michael Dukakis vetoed mandatory sentences for drug dealers,' says the deep-throated narrator. 'He vetoed the death penalty. His revolving-door prison policy gave weekend furloughs to first-degree murderers not eligible for parole. While out, many committed other crimes like kidnapping and rape and many are still at large. Now Michael Dukakis says he wants to do for America what he has done for Massachusetts. America can't afford that risk.' There is no mention of any one specific individual. Indeed, there is only one black prisoner in shot, though he is prominently walking to camera. The ad is a brilliant piece of propaganda. It is scary. The impression that dangerous prisoners are no sooner put into prison than they are automatically released must have had voters looking under their beds that night to check for released rapists.

Greg Stevens dislikes such analysis of the Media Team's ads – particularly analysis which examines an ad like the furlough one in terms of film criticism. 'People like you,' he told me, 'the media and other people involved in politics, ascribe much more Machiavellian motives to us than sometimes exist.' He claims that the 'look' of an individual ad is a product more of expediency than of intention. 'Sometimes we're doing something because of the time that it takes. You get up in the morning and the sun is on the other side of the building and so you do things differently.' If Stevens is correct – that many of the details in an ad are the product of accident – then surely political consultants are overcharging their clients? Or could it be that their clients know who to go to in order to get the production 'accident' they want?

Stevens and the Media Team are defensive about the furlough ad because of a potent accusation that has been levelled at them – racism. The truth of the matter is that some Republican voters *are* racist. The right-wing propagandist in America must make a delicate balance between creating sufficient concern (some say fear) in the white community about the threat of attack from black criminals or the threat of black workers taking white workers' jobs (an issue raised by arch-Republican Senator Jesse Helms in his last re-election campaign), whilst ensuring that neither the candidate nor the consultant is open to charges of racism. It may be that both candidates and consultants have erred too much on the side of caution in the past – the emergence of a Republican candidate like David Duke, a former Wizard of the Ku Klux Klan, demonstrates that there is a deep well of anti-black feeling to draw upon. Goebbels had the Jews to blame; the Republicans could have the blacks to blame – if they dare go that far.

Stevens points out that there is only one 'minority' (code for black)

107

prisoner featured in the furlough ad, substantially less than the number of blacks that should have been in the ad if the consultants had reflected the real proportion of blacks to whites in American jails. But alongside Stevens' own ad there were other, stronger ones made by so-called 'independent' groups which took head-on the issue of Willie Horton – ads which did not mince their words. The mainstream political consultants are legally obliged to exercise no influence over the content of ads made by these 'independent' groups. Such ads are often crude, often made by ad hoc groups who do not come forward to admit or defend authorship of the resulting work. As a consequence, Republican 'independent' groups during the 1988 election were not as sensitive in their approach to the race issue as the original furlough ad made by the Media Team had been.

There were two 'independent' ads made after the original furlough ad had been transmitted on television. Both featured victims of the Horton attack talking about their horrific experience; the suffering of these individuals is by implication placed squarely at the door of Michael Dukakis. Stevens claims he has not seen the ads, but accepts that 'my own taste is that this is probably on the line'. He says that because of Federal law he cannot call up the 'independent' groups and say 'Hey, that's a lousy ad', or 'That's a lousy idea, don't do it.'

The role of these 'independent' groups is going to become of greater and greater importance. Increasingly, they will be the shock troops of negative propaganda. The 'independent' ads can say things which for the mainstream consultants are unsayable. They can test the water, see just how crudely or viciously a particular allegation can be put before the public objects. Their very existence means that campaigns must get nastier still.

Counter-attack

How Dukakis should have countered the furlough ad and the 'independent' Horton ads was the great unanswered question of the 1988 Presidential propaganda campaign. Almost every Democratic consultant I spoke to had his own different theory – most developed around the theme of making an attack ad in response, showing that

Bush's own Republican state of Texas operated a similar furlough programme. But would this have worked? The central problem facing the candidate who is attacked is that it takes longer to explain the truth behind the accusation than it does to make the accusation in the first place. The response to the furlough ad could not, on television, be, 'Yes, the furlough programme did have its disappointments, but you have to put it in context. . . .' A newspaper article would, by comparison, *demand* such a format, but it is simply unworkable in the context of a thirty-second ad in which defence, in Ailes's words, is 'the weakest position'. Suppose Dukakis's response to the ad had gone along the lines of: 'This attack is unfair since my opponent operates a similar scheme.' That would appear to deal with the substance of the charge. But it doesn't, because Ailes's propaganda is an emotional attack designed to 'plug into' the voter's preconceived views. The voter would be ready to forgive a Republican a lapse on the furlough issue because everyone knows that Republicans are predisposed to be tough on crime. But they will hardly forgive a Democrat in such cricumstances, because the ad 'plugs into' their preconceived view that Democrats are soft on crime. So it is next to impossible for an adequate defence of the furlough ad to be mounted in the form of a thirty-second rebuttal. Thirty-second propaganda ads perfectly illustrate Mark Twain's axiom: 'A lie can travel around the world whilst the truth is putting its boots on.'

The question of how to respond to effective 'attack' ads therefore presents one of the most difficult challenges for the TV consultant. The obvious response – to answer the charges raised in the ad directly – is rarely successful. Probably the most skilful response to an attack, and one that played directly to the strengths of TV as a propaganda medium, was that developed by Jim Duffy for his candidate John Breaux who was standing for the Senate in Louisiana in 1986. Duffy got word that their opponent, the incumbent Senator Henson Moore, was planning to concentrate his attack on the fact that Breaux had missed a number of votes during his period of office as a Congressman – a total of 1083 votes, to be exact. Moore's consultant ran an ad which was based on the question: What does the number 1083 stand for? The ad featured a series of semi-humorous responses from ordinary voters (known in British television as 'vox pops') in which they guessed what the number 1083 actually represented. At the end of the ad the narrator's voice reveals that 1083 is in fact the number of votes that Duffy's candidate has missed – the 'number of times he didn't turn up for work'.

What would you have done if you were Duffy and had suffered such an attack? Perhaps your initial temptation would have been to show that, despite a poor attendance record, your candidate had accomplished a great deal. But this would be defensive, and you must never defend. Duffy followed a different course, and in the process unconsciously followed one of Goebbels's propaganda rules. He attacked. He turned the 1083 'attack' ad back on Moore and deliberately set out to confuse the voter by mimicking the exact style of the ad that his opposite number had made. Duffy's ad also starts by asking, 'What does the number 1083 stand for?' There then follows, in a replica of his opponent's ad, a series of 'vox pop' interviews before the narrator's voice reveals that 1083 is in fact the 'number of jobs lost in Louisiana each month because of Republican policies pursued by Henson Moore'. The two 1083 ads are hard to tell apart. One attacks Moore. One attacks Breaux. Moore's campaign team panicked and withdrew their ad – they couldn't take the risk that every time they were running their 1083 ad the voter was thinking that it was the other ad which attacked their own candidate.

Duffy's solution could only, of course, work on television. No attempt was made to answer the legitimate criticism made of Breaux's attendance record in Congress. Attack was demonstrably the best form of defence.

A funny attack

The future of negative television propaganda lies not in the harshness of the furlough ad, but in the use of another technique altogether – humour. We have already seen the importance that Roger Ailes places on humour in the context of the candidate's 'like quotient'. But humour is also a powerful method of attack. It may be hard to think of an answer to the furlough ad attack, but at least there is a grain of serious criticism in the work. Once someone starts to laugh at you, it's next to impossible to answer back.

One of Ailes's own most famous victories was achieved with the aid of humorous propaganda. In 1984 he was called in to run the campaign of Mitch McConnell, a Kentucky businessman who wanted to be Senator. The incumbent, Dee Huddlestone, was a well-liked Democrat, and Kentucky had been a Democrat state for years. When Ailes took over the campaign McConnell was forty-five points behind Huddlestone. Then Ailes's pollster, Janet Mullins, found what she called the 'magic bullet' lurking amongst the research. Huddlestone had travelled abroad to give speeches for money and had missed vital votes in the Senate as a consequence.

On learning of the 'magic bullet', Ailes devised the slapstick idea of a 'search' for Dee Huddlestone. His ad features a man holding a poster of Huddlestone, accompanied by a bloodhound, searching for the incumbent Senator – in a blatant pastiche of a warder from a chain gang looking for an escaped fugitive. Within days the voters were reacting in the way the politician most dreads – laughing at him. Huddlestone lost the election and Mitch McConnell became Senator.

Ailes's humorous Huddlestone ads are funny but crude. Production values are low, the ads are shot on videotape, and the camera-work and editing both lack sophistication. But not all consultants prefer their humour low-rent. Joe Slade-White is both a talented film-maker and at the cutting edge of humorous propaganda. He was responsible for what is probably the most devastating humorous ad of recent years.

Slade-White was brought in to devise ads in a 1986 race against the incumbent Mayor Pena of Denver. He and his team pored over the details of the polling looking for the potential 'partipulation' item, the 'magic bullet' in the data which matched the preconceived ideas in the voters' minds about the incumbent. The polls showed that Pena was perceived as imperious, isolated and egotistical. So Slade-White and his team looked for a detail in the life of the Mayor that illustrated a man with these negative qualities. 'I found this one small footnote,' says Slade-White. 'The Mayor had six bodyguards which cost the taxpayer $250,000. And the average voter was very afraid of walking the streets of Denver and being accosted by street gangs and they felt *they* weren't being protected. So I said, "Well, here's the Mayor who's protecting himself. He's out of touch. Let's see if we can show that."' Slade-White (of course) drew the inspiration for his ad from the world of entertainment television. 'About a week before, I had seen a *Monty Python* episode where they had used a group taking real small steps and moving like a mass. It was almost like a physical entity, and it was humorous physically. It was obviously a take-off on Chaplin and Buster Keaton and silent movies.' Then Slade-White made the connection with Mayor Pena. 'I said, "Wouldn't it be a humorous situation if you tried to imagine going through your daily life being surrounded by six bodyguards? What effect would it have on you?"'

Slade-White hired six tall male models, dressed them up in dark suits and aviator sunglasses so that they looked like secret service agents, and put a short actor in the middle of them to play the part of the Mayor. He then filmed a series of vignettes of normal everyday activities – shopping, jogging and playing baseball – with the six male models huddled tightly around the actor representing the Mayor and moving with him step by step. 'It was hilarious,' says Slade-White. 'I think we knew it was going to work even while we were shooting it. Sometimes you never know until you see it in the editing suite, but everyone on the crew was laughing.

Slade-White interspersed the individual comic scenes together with silent-movie type captions reading: 'The Mayor goes jogging' and 'The Mayor goes shopping'. There were no words on the soundtrack, only comic opera music. The ad is extremely funny and, like any comedy director of talent, Slade-White knows precisely why it is funny. He describes how he deliberately started the ad with moving shots showing the bodyguards darting past frame, followed by a static shot of the bodyguards huddled around second base on a baseball pitch. The shot holds a few seconds, and then a baseball is thrown from inside the phalanx of bodyguards to illustrate the Mayor playing baseball. What seems an arbitrary editing together of the scenes has been carefully thought out to create what Slade-White calls a 'laughter curve', peaking with the baseball shot and then 'keeping them laughing a little bit throughout, easing them down, so it's like a curve in terms of the laughter and the effect of it'.

The bodyguard ad is a wholly negative ad, yet it needs no words to make its attack. The Mayor simply *looks* ridiculous. So successful was the ad in capturing the mood of the voters of Denver that Slade-White's candidate, Don Bain, rose dramatically in the opinion polls and forced a 'run-off' against Mayor Pena, who eventually retained office only narrowly.

Slade-White's bodyguard ad is a pointer to the future of television propaganda. It is a negative, attacking piece of work that does not leave a nasty taste in the mouth of the voter. It appeals as much to an eight-year-old as it does to a thirty-eight-year-old. But, like almost all political propaganda, it leaves something crucial out – in this case the fact that Mayor Pena had received death threats from figures in organized crime. I put it to Joe Slade-White that he was turning an important issue – the protection of elected officials from potential assassins, into a joke. He answered that he had looked at the number of bodyguards other mayors had employed and had discovered that 'the Mayor of San Francisco only had two body-guards – and the previous Mayor of San Francisco had been assassinated'. Therefore the ostensible argument constructed by Slade-White to defend the legitimacy of his ad was that the *number* of bodyguards the Mayor employed was excessive. But this is disingenuous. Imagine a parallel – A humorous 'attack' ad on the President of America because of the number of secret service men hired to protect him. It would be considered in appalling taste and result in a massive negative backlash against the propagandist. The reaction of the voter would be: 'The President needs these men – people are out to kill him. Remember what happened to John Kennedy. Remember when Ronald Reagan was shot.'

The only reason Joe Slade-White's bodyguard ad worked as effectively as it did was because of the research that had been done beforehand. That is the key element – and it is an element the voter does not see. All the bodyguard ad was doing was *reinforcing* a preconceived idea expressed by the voters of Denver that their Mayor was aloof and out of touch. That is why in the end debate about the numbers of bodyguards the Mayor has is irrelevant. Once again the idea that the propagandist must 'canalize' an existing stream is shown to be a vital insight. It is the insight Goebbels had when isolating the Jews as his enemy; the insight Tony Schwartz had when creating *The Little Girl and the Daisy*; the insight Ailes and Atwater had when making the furlough ad; and exactly the same insight Joe Slade-White had when filming his bodyguard ad. The first and most vital aspect of attack propaganda is to find out what the ordinary citizen thinks, find out who they dislike and why, and then simply reinforce those feelings with your own propaganda.

How should the incumbent Mayor in Denver have dealt with Slade-White's brilliant propaganda attack? That is a question of such importance that it is the subject of academic study. For nothing reflects the growing status of the role of television propaganda in American society as much as the fact that the art of 'political consultancy' is now taught at American universities. At George Washington University in Washington DC I witnessed a group of postgraduate students animatedly discuss just what they would have done to counter Slade-White's ad. Their answers were most revealing.

The seminar was run by Dr Frank Luntz, a Republican consultant in his mid-twenties. Luntz showed the Slade-White bodyguard ad to his class and then asked for volunteers to role-play the Mayor – a part eventually taken by an earnest-looking student with thick glasses. When asked how he would have responded to the body-guard ad he replied, immediately and articulately, 'I think I'd do two things. I'd take advantage of both the paid and the free media. You run the paid part where you bring out the wife with the kids – maybe he's got grand-kids or something like that – and she talks about how she's making a sacrifice by allowing her husband to serve the city. Stress that there have been threats against his life and maybe she can get cherry-eyed or something like that. . . .' At which point Dr Luntz interrupted to say, 'You're the candidate and you're going to encourage your wife? "Honey please cry on television"?' The young student answered dismissively, 'I suspect that wouldn't be a problem because she's probably committed to helping him win,' before continuing, 'and I'd take advantage of the free media by marching out the chief of police, or somebody like that, and have them very soberly at a press conference detail point for point every single threat on your life. Maybe those that weren't specially legitimate. You name the date, you say this is when this threat was made. And you go right down the list, maybe they get one a week, one every couple of weeks. So you have the news detailing the fact that there have been threats on his life plus the commercials to demonstrate that the wife and kids do have a genuine concern there.'

The postgraduate student who was role-playing the part of the

Mayor was emphatic that the Mayor's wife was the best propaganda answer available. 'I think the Mayor inoculates himself by using the wife because the issue is that he's being self-centred and using taxpayer dollars to protect himself and it's not really protecting his family. But if you bring the wife on and you say "This is a member of my family" then the audience will relate to her and she'll make the link with the audience.'

At this point in the seminar Dr Luntz put a key question to his students. 'This is so manipulative. We're now thinking of ways to gather sympathy from the public. Is that what all this has become? If the wife has a broken leg are you going to highlight the cast? Are you going to make sure the dog is sitting in the commercial and have the husband pet it or something?' The students stared back at Dr Luntz, bemused. 'Of course,' their collective look of confusion seemed to say. 'We know this is manipulative – that's what we aspire to do, to manipulate people.'

That such a discussion could happen in a university of quality is enormously revealing – and the discussion itself is chiefly significant for what was *not* said. No one said that Slade-White's commercial was in any way harmful to the democratic system. No one thought that a thirty-second commercial which shows a tiny detail of a Mayor's record (and omits the key fact even about that tiny detail), and then goes on to ridicule him, using the values and the critical aspirations of a piece of comedy entertainment, was in any small way damaging to political life. These bright and gifted students, the elite of the American educational system, were so attuned to the nuances and internal dynamics of the political TV commercial that to question the bases on which the ad was formed would be to question the basis of the entire democratic system of America. 'This is the way it is,' they seemed to be saying. 'Why not go out and complain about the weather – you've as much chance of stopping it raining as you have of actually influencing the way these ads are constructed.'

The other fascinating point about this seminar is that the central reason why Slade-White's attack on the incumbent Mayor actually worked – that it was based on the previously held belief of the voters that the Mayor was distant and out of touch – was ignored. So the actual methods the students selected to deal with the attack were hardly adequate. Dealing with the *overt* issue – the bodyguards – would not have worked. As we have seen, it is easier to accuse than to defend on television, and the only way the Mayor could have adequately dealt with the attack would have been to deal with the issue underlying it – the issue of his own pomposity. How do you show in thirty seconds that you are not pompous? Perhaps make an ad showing you at a children's party getting a pie thrown in your face? But then the voters might think you are a fool, and your consultant would surely advise you that it is better to be perceived as pompous than risk being thought a fool. No, the case of Mayor Pena shows precisely why clever consultants believe that they should rarely answer the issues contained in a successful 'attack' ad. They should ignore it and attack their opponent themselves – attack him at his weakest point based on polling data.

The consequence of this logic, the almost slavish devotion to the Goebbels axiom of attack, means that the voter is left in a state of increasingly cynical confusion. During elections serious – albeit amusing – charges are laid via TV commercials against almost all candidates at every level of the American democratic process; charges which are rarely answered. The electoral waters are not so much muddied as turned jet-black. Is it surprising that many people simply do not bother to vote?

The British experience

In Britain in recent years there has been a reluctance to follow the American lead in the development of negative advertising. This has been for a number of reasons. First, the debate during election time in Britain is not dominated by the appearance of party election broadcasts; it is conducted more through 'unpaid' television news, current affairs programmes and national newspapers. Second, as discussed in Chapter 1, the party election broadcasts are both longer and less frequent than political adverts during an American Presidential election.

All this means that propaganda attacks in Britain, when they come, tend to have more substance than their American counterparts. Commercials like the furlough ad or the bodyguard ad would have a hard time working here because, as Sir Tim Bell said in another context, the danger is that the press would 'take your trousers down'. This is not to say that there has not been some memorable negative advertising – we have already mentioned Saatchi's famous cinema ad showing a long queue of people together with the slogan 'Labour isn't working'. But this ad was based on perceived voter dissatisfaction with the high rate of unemployment rather than concentrating on one tiny fact to represent the whole. Labour did target Mrs Thatcher's alleged intransigence during the 1987 General Election – one of their most effective posters showed a picture of Thatcher with the slogan 'Try telling her anything' – but again, this propaganda concentrated on a broad issue of voter concern. The equivalent propaganda technique to a Joe Slade-White ad would have been to search through Mrs Thatcher's record for a tiny, apparently trivial, issue that showed up her perceived intransigence and highlight that. At the 1987 election this might have involved, for example, concentrating on Thatcher's bizarre use of the royal 'we' to describe herself, as in the famous line 'We are a grandmother.' An American consultant could easily have made a humorous ad highlighting such pomposity. But you couldn't run such an ad for five minutes, the minimum length currently used for party politicals, which is why the cleverest British political propaganda is to be seen on posters and not on TV. The famous poster carrying the slogan 'Labour's policy on arms' under a picture of a soldier with his hands up, made by Saatchi's in 1987, and the poster of Norman Lamont, the Conservative Chancellor, dressed as 'Vatman', produced by the Shadow Communications Agency in 1992, show a wit and sophistication seldom seen in British TV propaganda. However, there is no reason why British political propagandists cannot apply the American TV lessons of attack to their poster campaigns, and search for the apparently trivial negative detail in their opponent's character which plugs into the predisposition of the electorate.

Focus in attack propaganda is just as vital for British propagandists as it is for their American cousins. The Labour party victory at the by-election at Monmouth in the spring of 1991 showed how, by concentrating on a single issue – in this case the alleged 'privatization' of the National Health Service, Labour's propaganda could be extremely successful. This by-election victory, orchestrated to a large extent by Peter Mandelson, shows graphically how the media themselves can be influenced to concentrate on one simple issue.

The main problem that the British propagandist faces in this area is how to respond to attacks. In Britain the political divide between the major parties means that there is a massive predisposition amongst the electorate to believe certain facts about each party: for example, that the Conservatives will lower taxes and that the Labour party will spend more on the National Health Service. So each party in its attacks tries to 'partipulate' into the negative aspect of their opponent's policies. Thus the Conservatives concentrate on showing how Labour will raise taxes, while Labour concentrate on showing that the Conservatives have run down the National Health Service. But how should each party respond to such attacks? The lesson that the British propagandist should learn from the experience of Mayor Pena and his bodyguards is that politicians should never *voluntarily* waste valuable propaganda time defending their weak policy areas (though they may be forced to by the 'unpaid' media), because on such issues voter predisposition is so strong that nothing said in propaganda terms will be believable.

The truth of this proposition was borne out by the way attack issues developed during the 1992 British General Election. Predictably Labour attacked the Tories over the condition of the National Health Service and the Conservatives mounted their main attack on Labour over their proposed tax increases.

Labour, like the Conservatives, used a feature film director to make their most important party election broadcast. Mike Newell, director of *Dance With A Stranger*, made the now infamous ad which dramatically portrayed the case of two children, suffering from glue ear. The parents of one of them could afford to pay for private treatment in order to circumvent the National Health waiting list, the others could not. The case of the girl who had to wait for treatment on the National Health Service was intended to be taken as representing an amalgam of similar cases – although it later transpired the film *was* loosely based on one particular case. This was the first non-biographical election broadcast to overcome the problem of sustaining an emotional impact for ten minutes. It achieved its success by concentrating on a dramatic story. There was no need for commentary – just music and emotion.

Unfortunately for Labour, and Philip Gould (a leading member of Labour's communications team and the man who had the idea for the film), the message was quickly lost in an acrimonious row over who had leaked to the press the name of the little girl on whose experience the film had been roughly based. Even though Tory Central Office eventually admitted that they had had a role in putting the little girl's hospital consultant in touch with the *Daily Express*, the row could only have benefited the Conservatives since it focused the debate away from the central issue of the funding of the Health Service.

William Waldegrave, the then Health secretary, likened the Labour election broadcast to a Nazi propaganda film. He was closer to the truth than perhaps he realised, for Goebbels would have heartily approved of the film's technique. It was unintellectual, emotive and avoided any discussion of the actual issue. Perhaps the most significant lesson to be learnt from the transmission of this, the most American in style of Election Broadcasts, was the extensive controversy it caused in the press. Nothing could have shown more clearly the fact that whilst it is easy to import American techniques of communication, it is altogether much harder to prevent British journalists questioning their validity.

In an interview during the election John Major remarked that when voters were asked in a non-political way about the quality of the Health Service people conceded that it had improved, and it was simply only in the context of Labour's constant attacks that the Tories could not win the debate. Which is why the wisest course of action the Tories could take was not to defend their Health policy but to attack the opposition at their weakest point – tax.

After the election one leading figure in the Labour party revealed to me that one propaganda poster had been responsible for sinking Labour's campaign. The poster showed the silhouette of a huge bomb against a red background. Written on the bomb were the words, '*Labour's tax bombshell. You'd pay £1,250 more tax a year under Labour.*' At the bottom of the poster, in small letters, was the sentence, '*Labour's manifesto promises would cost the average tax-payer an extra £1,250 a year.*' This same leading Labour figure told me that he had been campaigning in a council-run old people's home when a little old lady had leant forward to him and said: 'I'd like to see a Labour government, it's just that I can't afford to pay all that extra tax.'

The old lady's remarks are testimony to the power of the Conservatives' propaganda. For no matter how hard the Labour party talked of the fact that the average man or woman would in fact benefit from their tax proposals, the predisposition in the voter's mind was that Labour was the party of higher taxes – higher taxes for everyone. As Peter Walker remarked ruefully after the votes were counted, 'The wallet does speak' at election time.

So what could Labour have done differently? In a way they were as stuck as Mayor Pena was with his bodyguard problem. The only way they could have countered the predisposition in the voter's mind that their party was one of tax increases for all, would have been to demonstrate total financial rectitude. They went some way towards this in the person of the shadow chancellor, John Smith, who was consistently spoken of by voters as a more popular potential chancellor than Norman Lamont. Unfortunately for Labour, the Tory tax attack went in tandem with attacks on the competence of the then Labour leader, Neil Kinnock. Inevitably, given Britain's Tory-dominated tabloid press, Kinnock was the victim of much abuse. But the abuse, attempting to show the Labour leader as a lightweight untrustworthy windbag, would not have worked had it not 'partipulated' into similar views the voters themselves held about Neil Kinnock. It was this combination of attacks, on taxation and on the Labour leader personally as unfit to govern, that was so effective. The Tory poster claiming that the average person would pay more in tax under Labour 'partipulated' into the voter's concern about Neil Kinnock. The reasoning the Tories aimed to plant in the average voter's mind was, 'Even if Labour say they aren't going to increase the taxes of the average working man, one look at Kinnock and you just simply can't believe it.'

A member of the Conservative communication team put it to me this way: 'When we knew Maggie was a liability we ditched her. That way the voters think they've had a change already. Now if Labour had been as ruthless as we were and ditched Kinnock and put in Smith before the election then a lot of our attacks on Labour simply wouldn't have worked.' The Tories feared that John Smith's sober, trustworthy image would have rendered their attack propaganda on Labour's tax plans ineffective. The irony of this logic is that it was Smith himself who pressed for Labour's tax plans to be as harsh as they were. But, as always, in the world of attack propaganda appearance, not substance, is all.

Notes

1. Meissner, Hans Otto: *Magda Goebbels – The First Lady of the Third Reich*

2. Quoted in Diamond, Edwin, and Stephen Bates: *The Spot – The Rise of Political Advertising on Television*

Chapter Five

Getting on the News

Josef Goebbels faced many problems, but he never had to face the biggest difficulty that today's democratic propagandists confront: they do not have total control over the media. Television news and current affairs programmes often insist on doing what propagandists consider an unpardonable sin – setting their own agenda. So how can the propagandist try to retain control?

In the ranks of today's democratic propagandists there is one man who more than any other has succeeded in influencing the national news channels of the world's biggest television democracy. He is the man who was Ronald Reagan's closest communications adviser during the early White House years, a man who operated with the deliberately understated title of Deputy Chief Of Staff. He is a man who perfectly encapsulates the modern philosophy of television-based propaganda. He is a man who has always been perfectly honest and open about the fact that he is not an adviser on the 'issues'; a man from whom all aspiring propagandists can learn. His name is Michael Deaver.

After a decade rich in incident, Deaver now operates out of a smart suite of offices on K Street in Washington's Georgetown. I first met him over lunch in a bistro on nearby M Street – a lunch during which Deaver, honest about the fact that he is a 'reformed alcoholic', was careful to drink only iced water. When I questioned him about an anecdote that I had heard attributed to him he was equally honest in his reply. 'I may have said it. Because of the drink there's things I can't remember saying now.' But do not be deceived. This is a man who is as sharp about the principles of television propaganda as ever.

Michael Deaver was raised in a lower middle-class home in California. After majoring in political science at college he joined the Republican party. Eventually in 1966, at the age of twenty-eight, through his association with William Clark who became the Governor's Chief of Staff, he met the man on whom he was to have such an influence – the then Governor of California, Ronald Reagan. Deaver started by organizing Reagan's press appearances, and soon a special relationship developed which was to profit them both.

Though Deaver started work for Reagan in 1966 it was not until ten years later, in 1976, that both of them were involved in a national campaign when Reagan stood for the Republican nomination for President, losing narrowly to Gerald Ford. By the time that campaign was over Deaver had developed firm opinions about the future of Reagan's propaganda. 'I understood that the evening news was where 80 per cent of the American public was getting all of its information about its candidates,' says Deaver, 'and it was making up its mind about what they said and how they moved and how they reacted from television – not from newspapers or from debates or political literature.' Deaver is a realist. He is a man who, having seen how the media land lay, accepted it and adapted to it. And he learned one great truth, a truth that Goebbels had first discovered nearly fifty years earlier. 'When we ran again in 1979,' says Deaver, 'I really dedicated all of my time to being sure that all the space around the head was filled with something that was going to be pleasant and entertaining. And if I could do that, the television producers would put it on television. Because they're not in the news business, they're in the entertainment business. And they're in the business to make money. And if I could become a good producer they were going to buy my product. So I wasn't so interested in what the candidate was saying – there were a lot of people that worried about that, including the candidate. What I was interested in was filling up all that space that came into the living room with something that would be, one, attractive enough to make people watch it, and two – amplify visually what he was saying.'

123

Deaver decided that the route to being the best propagandist for Reagan was to become the best TV producer in America. He began to look at every political situation with the eyes of a TV producer, a view coloured with his newly found belief that television journalists were kidding themselves that they were in the news business – they were actually in the entertainment business.

After the election of Reagan in 1980 Deaver unconsciously followed another rule of Goebbels's – simplify and focus.

'When I was there in the first four and a half years,' says Deaver, 'you started with a basic theme of the Reagan Presidency, which was economic recovery. And I can remember in the first year and a half telling everybody in the White House: "Don't bring me anything to go on the President's schedule unless it's got to do with economic recovery – because it's not going to get on there."' Deaver constantly refers to the importance of 'themes'. As explained in Chapter 3, today's propagandist prefers 'themes' to 'issues'. Promises on issues can get the candidate into trouble – they are too specific; a promise based on a 'theme', however, is much safer. 'It's morning again in America' is a theme; 'Let's cut welfare' is an issue.

'So you started with basic themes that were set by the President himself,' says Deaver. 'It was economic recovery. It was peace through strength – or whatever it was that he'd outlined. And then we would take a look at the outside forces that would dictate or affect our schedule. What the Congress was doing. What foreign governments were doing. Which other people were going to be in town creating news and that sort of thing. And we'd chart out for six to eight weeks at a time what we wanted to do, knowing that all the time there'd be all this stuff coming at us. We wanted to set out where we wanted to be four to six weeks from now and we would plan an event based on that very day. To build on the story.'

So obsessed was he with the visual element of television that he became known as 'Mike, the Vicar of the Visuals'. Deaver told me a story about housing starts – the number of new houses whose construction had begun – which shows just why he inspired such a title. He was aware that when Reagan took over the Presidency there was double digit inflation and high unemployment, and that consequently political havoc was caused by the President's austerity measures. Deaver was waiting for a sign that the tide had turned, that the economic indicators were starting to show recovery. Then 'the economic people came in my office one morning and said, "Housing starts are going up." Now when housing starts or automobile sales begin to go up in this country, that means we're really starting to get confidence back in our economy. And what they suggested we do that morning was to take the President down to the Press Room in the White House and make this announcement. And I said, "No, let's not do that. Let somebody go out and find me the five cities in America where housing starts are going up faster than they are any place else and bring those back to me." They brought them back and we took a look at them and we decided on Fort Worth, Texas. The next day we flew the President of the United States and a planeload of press out there, and he made the announcement about housing starts. Now the difference was that when that guy was sitting there watching television that night, when he was watching the evening news, he didn't see the President of the United States in a business suit with the Presidential seal behind him. What he saw was the President of the United States with a couple of guys in hard hats in a framed-out house and he says: "What's the old man doing in that construction project?" And then he listens a minute and he says, "Housing starts are going up. Things must be getting better." You see, that picture was filled with a visual story that amplified what the news was.'

Deaver proudly boasts that he was 'hard put' not to find a visual for any particular event. But he candidly admits that if he couldn't find the right visual then 'we wouldn't do it. The visual's too important.' This is revealing, for it shows that the President of the United States's movements were not determined by which action was more important for the political life of the nation; his actions were determined by which activities could provide the best visual for the television news.

There were a number of other consequences of Deaver's insistence on the visual element in any activity relating to the President. Not only was the illusion created that Reagan was dynamic, constantly out and about mingling with ordinary Americans, but it enabled him to be protected from TV journalists. If the President was actually involved in action, there could be no place for formal questions challenging what he was doing. Journalists might try and shout questions to provoke an answer, but that was easily handled – Reagan could answer only those questions he chose to, whilst the journalists themselves appeared gauche and unsophisticated.

Sam Donaldson, ABC's White House correspondent during the Reagan years, was one of the journalists who most objected to the way Deaver orchestrated the propaganda of the President. He became famous for shouting questions at Reagan during the carefully choreographed Deaver visuals. Donaldson thinks Deaver 'didn't care about the issues and he didn't care about the words'. Donaldson recalls that, during the 1984 Presidential campaign, 'I remember many times talking about shortcomings, in a sense of policies that were not working, or about Presidential statements that just didn't bear a relationship to the facts. But what you were seeing – because we are on television – was this smiling, genial grandfather figure, this John Wayne character. And you were not hearing a thing I said because when the eye and ear conflict the eye always wins. The thing you want to try and do in television is put the two of them together, but if a Deaver gives you only pictures that show "Morning in America", your complaint that beneath the "Morning" there's an open sewer is going to be lost. No one pays any attention to the words – just the music.'

Dottie Lynch of CBS tells how 'Leslie Stahl [CBS's former White House Correspondent] did a very negative story on President Reagan saying all these things that he had done badly, and the pictures were all of blue skies and American flags and Reagan against this backdrop. And she got off the air and said, "Oh gosh, they're gonna hate me," and then got a call from somebody at the White House saying, "That was the best piece we ever had", and she said "What do you mean?" They said, "The pictures were absolutely beautiful." And for a while I think a lot of people were manipulated very willingly by Michael Deaver and the Reagan administration because they knew television wanted pictures.'

Deaver was the first modern propagandist fully to realize the extent to which the TV networks would be passively grateful if he attempted to do their job for them. Larry Speakes, the then White House Press Secretary, is quoted as saying that the first question the TV networks asked of any proposed event was: 'Are there any pictures?' Deaver reasoned that it was in the interest of both the

President and the TV networks for him to provide the pictures they craved. And in successfully doing so he proved his own axiom – that the TV networks were operating at the level of entertainers rather than journalists.

Michael Deaver's propaganda followed (again, albeit unconsciously) the classic Goebbels formula: entertain, and repeat. 'Now one thing that I learned in the White House,' says Deaver, 'was that you cannot get across a feeling or a position to the American public without repetition. You can't – and some politicians do – talk about the environment one day and education the next day and have any meaningful impact on what's going to happen.'

Deaver repeated the same message so often that it even caused Reagan (whom Deaver has been known to refer to as 'the talent') problems. 'In 1983 I looked at some of the research,' says Deaver, 'and saw that one of the largest negatives against Ronald Reagan after three years in the White House was the fact that people thought – about 70 per cent of the people thought – he had not done a good job in the field of education. Now forget that the President of the United States has very little to do with education in this country. People still thought he hadn't done a good job. For six weeks we went across this country and at least three days out of all those six weeks he made the same speech over and over again – in different venues. One time in a school yard, one time in a classroom, one time in a tech centre, one time in a meeting of college administrators. But it was basically the same speech over and over again. To the point where he said to me, "I'm not gonna give this speech any more – everyone's heard it", and I said, "No, they haven't. Not yet." At the end of that six weeks he had reversed the negatives. He now had a 70 per cent positive on what the American people thought his role in education was.'

Deaver thus managed to create an illusion of activity in an area where he knew the President's powers were themselves illusory. Goebbels himself would have been proud of such an achievement. Pause also to reflect that this particular method of repetition has only been made possible because of television. For this is a very different technique from the repetition of the old standard 'stump' speech, where the candidate would make much the same speech in much the same type of location. Here is a case of a President making a speech on a specific issue where the key is the *visual* backdrop he is speaking against. The audience at home is not supposed to listen to the words of the President, they are supposed to register a feeling that the President is concerned. Deaver, like Goebbels, succeeded in using a visual medium successfully to short-circuit the voter's rational perceptions and substituted an emotional response to the picture.

Only now, looking back, do some of the top editorial figures in TV news admit that Deaver exploited the networks. Dottie Lynch told me, 'In the beginning of the Reagan administration Deaver was a genius at being able to manipulate and work with television news before television news really understood that it was being used in this way.' But just what could the networks have done about Deaver? Donaldson believes they had few options, since Deaver was able to operate as he did because he controlled *access* to the President. Access was the key. Deaver knew that the network news correspondents were paid a fortune in order to show the President. Mark Hertsgaard, in his powerful indictment of journalism during the Reagan Presidency, *On Bended Knee*, quotes Deaver as saying: 'My position was "Screw 'em!" . . . I mean we've got the horse. They're getting paid $150,000 a year to cover the President of the United States.'[1] Donaldson, one of the most tenacious White House correspondents of the period, still recalls with some force how Deaver attempted to manipulate the networks by coming up with what he called the 'story of the day'. 'They would have a meeting at eight o'clock in the morning,' says Donaldson, 'and decide what they wanted the story of the day to be and how they would control it. The meetings that had to do with the story of the day they would open to the press. They would let the cameras in. They would have this little stilted conversation that Ronald Reagan would go through, but we would have it. And the meetings that had to do with subjects that we might have thought were important ones but they didn't want on air they would close. So there would be no access. And they controlled Reagan's movements so that on the days when he had something they wanted him to say he would be walking where the press could question him and on days when they didn't want him to say anything we'd never see him.'

What can a TV producer do when confronted with such a

situation? If Deaver was wrong, and these were journalists rather than purveyors of entertainment, wouldn't they have created their own agenda rather than tamely following the one laid down by the propagandists? Donaldson, a man who resolutely classes himself as a hard journalist, disagrees. 'As a reporter you try to gain access, but if the door is shut you can't break it down – particularly if you're talking about a President. There are too many people with guns and badges to keep you from doing that. If you try to control the agenda as a reporter you're gonna fail, because the agenda is not driven by the press.' Donaldson says he is constantly asked, 'Why don't you set the agenda?' and answers wearily, 'If I cover your campaign I need to report on what you are doing and saying. It's not up to me to be the campaign manager.' He believes that 'If I were representing a third party I might say, "You, Mr President, will discuss the environment today because it's important", but as a reporter, unless I can question him on the subject – and access is everything – I don't have the opportunity to do that. So you pretty much cover the campaigns as the candidates play it out. If the candidates want to talk about the issues, the press is gonna talk about the issues. If the candidates want to go to a flag factory, the press is going to show a flag factory. The democratic process is not helped by the flag factory.'

Donaldson skates over the issue of connivance – but that there was a cosy, symbiotic relationship between the White House and the correspondents there can be no doubt. This complicity between the networks and Michael Deaver to produce good visuals reached a peak during Reagan's visit to Normandy in 1984 – the fortieth anniversary of D-Day. Deaver confesses that the whole event was 'choreographed' in advance as a result of detailed discussions with the network producers. 'Every one of those producers would have gone with us on the pre-advance and the advance and they would have worked with us.' Deaver told me that the whole of the two-hour ceremony was designed around the mutually agreed five or six 'visually attractive events' that would take place during the day.

Months of preparation went into the event. Deaver walked the beaches with the television producers to make sure they all agreed on the ideal visual, with Deaver learning exactly what picture was going to be on which camera at what time. He was under no illusions as to the attention span of the audience, and organized a 'mix of various events at one spot so that we could interest the television people in covering it for a period of time'. Deaver also knew that a desirable ingredient in every television entertainment is drama. So he imported drama into the event. The White House ensured that some of the survivors of the assault on the beaches, the famed 'Boys of Point Du Roc', were flown over, and that the TV producers knew where they were sitting. He also had an American woman flown out by military transport because she had written to the President about the gallant actions of her father, and he made sure that the TV people could cut to her at the key moment in Reagan's speech when he referred to her.

As I watched a tape of the news report of the Normandy celebrations alongside Michael Deaver it was hard to believe that he had not actually produced the news himself. 'As you can see,' he said, pointing to the woman who had written to the President, 'she's very emotional at this point, as was the President. The President always liked the ability to be able to respond to a citizen and so he would forever be bringing these letters to us that he'd want to read in his speeches – and it was also great television.' Great television – that was always Deaver's aim.

Deaver did not create the symbiotic relationship between the networks and the White House; he merely exploited it and took it to new heights. In this he was aided by a series of historical coincidences. He had at his disposal a President who was not just a professional performer, but a man who craved direction; a President, moreover, whom people warmed to, who was quintessentially likeable; a President who preferred the glamorous ceremonial tasks of his office as head of state (tasks which in Britain are devolved to the monarch) rather than the tedious deal-making which is often the everyday lot of the powerful politician. Furthermore, Deaver was working with a press corps which contained some members who felt deferential to this President. 'You must remember,' one correspondent told me, 'we'd had a decade of bad-news Presidents in the seventies, and some of us felt maybe a little guilty about the way we'd gone about attacking them during this period.' Deaver was also hugely helped by the increasing necessity of the American networks to compete with satellite and cable channels. The networks' audience share and revenue were falling. They needed the news to boost their ratings. And how do you boost ratings? By entertainment, of course, and Michael Deaver was there to help them in their aim.

It was fitting that the man who had benefited so much from the power of the visual image should have been almost broken by the choice of a bad visual image. For the story of Deaver's error at Bitburg is almost more indicative of the way television propaganda images work than the story of any of his successes. Deaver went in 1984 to what was then West Germany to prepare for another television event spectacular – the television reconciliation between Germany and America forty years after the end of the Second World War. The broad 'theme' of Deaver's proposal for the President's trip was one of 'reconciliation in Europe'. One of the visuals Deaver was working on involved a visit to a German war cemetery so that Reagan could lay a wreath. Bitburg cemetery was covered in snow the day that Deaver inspected it on the advance visit. He now says his instinct was to order all the graves in the cemetery to be checked out, but he contented himself with turning to one of the German officials who was accompanying him and asking whether there were any 'problems' in the graveyard. Deaver still says, in almost tortured terms, 'I should have been more careful.' Deaver's big mistake was exposed months before the trip actually went ahead. Buried in the cemetery at Bitburg were forty-nine members of the Second Waffen SS Panzer Division. There was uproar in America from the Jewish community, but Reagan refused to cancel his visit. The German government put pressure on the White House to go ahead as scheduled, saying it would be an almost unpardonable sin to humiliate Chancellor Kohl by refusing his invitation to visit the site. To appease the critics a visit to the concentration camp of Bergen-Belsen was hastily added to the itinerary, and the President went ahead and visited Bitburg.

More than half a dozen years on, Deaver is still upset about Bitburg; without hesitation he considers it his greatest mistake. Over lunch during my first meeting with him he seemed close to tears when talking about the incident. He clearly felt he had failed the President in a fundamental way. 'But surely,' I said, 'isn't this all out of proportion?' Bitburg was a purely visual event. Less than 2 per cent of the soldiers buried in the cemetery had been members of the Waffen SS. Other Western leaders had laid wreaths there before.

No one could ever suggest that President Reagan was in any way empathizing with the SS or with the values they represented. The SS men were even buried in a different part of the cemetery, and there was no question of Reagan laying a wreath on their particular graves. Deaver might, I suggested, like to consider that in the great scheme of his communications work this was a rather trivial episode. 'Trivial?' he repeated incredulously. 'It certainly wasn't trivial to the American Jewish leadership.' Deaver clearly believes that his failure to notice those Waffen SS graves at Bitburg was a massive blot on his otherwise illustrious communications career. It represents a kind of ironic justice that Deaver is concerned not about any failure of apparent substance, but with a failure of impression, a failure of image. The TV image of Reagan presented at Bitburg was not a successful one.

The fact that Deaver is still so upset about it all demonstrates that to him *everything* was image. The very word 'image' is almost pejorative now; journalists talk of 'image consultants' as if they work at the margins of power, as if 'image' is at the opposite end of the spectrum of importance from 'substance'. What the Bitburg episode shows is that, where television propaganda is concerned, 'image' *is* the substance of the message.

This assertion that in television propaganda 'image' is 'substance' is further illustrated by Deaver's explanation of how he handled the type of events that *had* to be shown, but which in his ideal world would have been kept off the President's schedule. For instance, Deaver always fought against any suggestion that Reagan participate in the launching of ships or planes, because 'one of Ronald Reagan's largest negatives was that people thought he was more likely to get us into a war'. None the less, other advisers prevailed when Reagan agreed to visit a factory making giant bombers for the US Air Force. Deaver's solution to the potential image problem of allowing a picture of Reagan to be shown next to a huge bomber was to order a large sign reading 'Prepared for Peace' to be draped over one side of the hangar behind the plane. Deaver's standing joke with Bill Hinkle, head of the advance team, was, 'If you can't give me a good visual, give me a big sign.'[2] Deaver told me, 'If we were going to have to do this kind of event then I wanted to be sure that everybody understood that we were building these aeroplanes because Ronald

Reagan believed that peace came through strength. Just one more time to emphasize that theme.'

All the propaganda lessons that Deaver learned in Reagan's first term in the White House came together in his policy directives for the Presidential campaign of 1984, directives which made that campaign probably the most masterly re-election operation ever run. The key to its success was the extension of Deaver's workaday policy of limiting the type of access to the President that correspondents got. Deaver reasoned that, 'All the Presidents in the last half-century in this country who've got into trouble were people who were unable to plan and look ahead for a few weeks, and when they got behind the media got them or Congress got them or somebody else that was opposed to them got them on the defensive.' No one, vowed Deaver, was going to do that to his President. So he limited the number of news conferences which Reagan gave during the 1984 campaign: limited them to just *one*. There has never been a campaign before or since in the television age in which the President so rarely answered reporters' questions. Indeed, even the one news conference that Reagan gave during the campaign was not actually on the subject of the election, but as Donaldson says, 'He took some questions and we managed to question him to some extent on the budget deficit and some of the questions that his opponent Walter Mondale had been raising. But other than that he held no news conferences and we would shout at him as he went to the helicopter. This, of course, was no substitute for the kind of questioning that should have gone on on a daily basis – and that Mondale had to be subjected to. You know, if you're in the White House as the incumbent you can control these things so much better. You're on a platform where secret service are around you and where you can claim that affairs of state keep you from meeting the press.'

Whilst not necessarily denying that his chief aim had been to keep Reagan away from the press, Deaver is somewhat jaundiced about the right of correspondents like Donaldson to take the moral high ground. A natural consequence of his belief that journalists are in the entertainment business is that he regards any of their criticisms as the kind that entertainers might make. He believes that the White House press corps were a cosseted group of people who *themselves* wanted to be on television each night. To him the logic of

133

their complaint was simple: if they didn't have access to the President, then they themselves couldn't get on TV. That, he felt, was the motivation for such complaints as Donaldson's – not some great concern about the nature of democracy in America. 'It was very frustrating for those fellows whose contracts depend upon how many times they got on television every night,' admits Deaver. 'And yes, the President was not available for them. But they could get their questions answered by me or Jim Baker or the press office or anybody else. The facts were out. It was just that they didn't get their "sound bite" on television every night.'

The brilliance of Deaver's tactic of restricting reporters' access to Reagan was that it in no way influenced how often the President was seen on television. Deaver carried on organizing stunning visuals for the TV producers throughout the campaign. The voters could *see* the President as much as they liked. They just couldn't hear him answer many questions. And if he didn't answer questions how could he make a mistake? How could he say something silly which would jeopardize the campaign? The TV viewer of the 1984 campaign was left with the impression of Walter Mondale on the defensive each night, answering questions which reporters had put to him on their own terms. The juxtaposition with the controlled, dynamic Reagan of the Deaver visual was devastating.

Other political consultants saw what Deaver had managed to do and they liked what they saw. Raymond Strother came to believe that it might be possible to run a Presidential campaign without any 'paid' advertising at all. 'I actually wrote a memo in 1986 or 1987 for Gary Hart about our next campaign, where I suggested that perhaps we didn't need paid television. That we should look very hard at – because the networks cover the election so very well – utilizing their talent and their brains. For example, coming up with situations that would follow the candidate delivering his message in a natural setting and give it to America inexpensively, free. George Bush went to a flag factory and people said "What the hell is George Bush doing in a flag factory?" Well, if there was something wrong with it why were there a hundred cameras behind George Bush filming him in the flag factory? And what did the flag factory say? "I'm a patriot. Mabye my opponent isn't a patriot."'

But how do you get the networks to cover your candidate if he is unknown? Dottie Lynch reveals one technique which she used when she too was working for Gary Hart, though in 1983 when he was relatively unknown. 'If Reagan would make a statement on whatever – soup kitchens or poverty – Hart would then be ready to respond and "play into" the story that was going to be covered.' 'Playing in' to the story meant trying to get their candidate to appear in a visual which fitted into the agenda set by the politician whose actions they knew would be covered. Thus if Reagan made a speech about poverty, Gary Hart would be asked by his propagandists to hold a photo-opportunity in a soup kitchen in the hope that the networks would use the pictures of Hart in connection with the agenda set by Reagan.

Why do the broadcasters succumb to this sort of manipulation? Only for one simple reason – it makes 'good television'. And the criteria of what makes a good TV news item has been changing. Kiku Adatto's research work has shown how the length of the 'sound bite' – the amount of time a politician is shown speaking on the news – has decreased.[3] In 1968 the average sound bite was 42.2 seconds, while in 1988 it was 9.8 seconds. As a former CBS correspondent called Fred Graham wrote recently: 'News stories at CBS tended to become two-minute morality plays, with heroes or villains and a tidy moral, to be summed up at the end.'[4] Michael Deaver, with his belief in 'entertaining' news visuals, must have been pushing against an open door when trying to get the networks to act at his behest.

Much of the blame for the atmosphere of negativity and triviality which surrounds many TV election campaigns is laid by Roger Ailes squarely at the feet of the networks and their constant search for the best visual.[5] 'It's my orchestra pit theory of politics,' he says. 'If you have two guys on a stage and one guy says, "I have a solution to the Middle East problem', and the other guy falls in the orchestra pit, who do you think is going to be on the evening news?' At a seminar held at the Barone Center at Harvard University after the 1988 election Ailes was pressed on such views by Judy Woodruff, who said to him, 'So you're saying the notion of the candidate saying, "I want to run for President because I want to do something for the country" is crazy?' Ailes answered with one word: 'Suicide.'

Ailes's 'orchestra pit' theory is a dangerous one for any proponent of an informed democracy – dangerous particularly because it may be true. For isn't it inevitable that a news programme chasing ratings will concentrate on the entertaining visual story before anything else? And won't the clever propagandist realize that the way to expose his opponent is not to show the fallacies in his argument, but rather to place a banana skin under his shoe whilst the news cameras are running?

This proposal is not as facetious as it sounds. Remember Gerald Ford stumbling as he descended the steps of a plane? That image came to haunt him as evidence that here there really was a President who could not walk and chew gum at the same time. Or Jimmy Carter collapsing whilst running a mini-marathon? Is there a better pictorial representation of a beleaguered President than the sight of Carter practically on his knees with exhaustion? Or Michael Dukakis allowing himself to be photographed by the news cameras as he drove a tank? That image started as a photo-opportunity which became an advert for the Democrats, which became a news story, which then turned up as an 'attack' ad for the Republicans. The visual image of the perceived liberal in an instrument of war created such dissonance that it came to epitomize Dukakis's botched campaign.

What would Lincoln have made of all this? In an age before television, whether the candidate accidentally slipped on the way to the podium or not was no guide to his fitness for high office. Recently the fact that George Bush had food poisoning in Japan led the TV news. But the question that broadcasters have to ask themselves is, would such a story have led the news *if there had been no pictures*? And if the answer is 'No', then Ailes really has exposed a complicity between propagandist and broadcaster to go for the image at the expense of the editorial merit of the story.

At its most devastating, one TV image can destroy a man's political career. The worst TV image Deaver recalls of the Reagan years was not the sight of poor Walter Mondale limping his way through the campaign of 1984. It was of an altogether more dramatic moment, which occurred three years earlier in the White House just after Reagan had been shot on 30 March 1981. Alexander Haig, Reagan's Secretary of State, rushed into the press room and stood perspiring in front of the microphone. 'I am in control here,' he announced, 'pending the return of the Vice-President.' The words — even though they inaccurately represented the chain of command — were not the problem. It was the *image* which Haig presented to the television world. When the TV viewer wanted an appearance of calmness and quiet confidence, Haig came over like the mad general out of *Dr Strangelove*. Deaver is caustic about Haig's performance. It was precisely the sort of situation in which he would never have allowed Reagan to appear (equally, it was precisely the sort of a situation in which a competent TV producer would never allow his TV presenter to appear).

Deaver's criticism of Haig was that of a TV professional, not a politician. But we should expect that. As Peggy Noonan wrote, 'The president's top aides . . . were the line producers of the show called the "White House", with Ronald Reagan as the president. And this wasn't particular to that White House, it was simply a trend that achieved its fullness in the Reagan era.'[6]

The British experience

British politics have never seen a propagandist with the gifts and influence of Michael Deaver. Part of the reason is structural. Responsibility for each Prime Minister's relationship with the press is split between the individual party's Director of Communications (which is a political appointment) and the press officer of Number 10 Downing Street (which is a civil service appointment). Under Mrs Thatcher's pugnacious press officer, Sir Bernard Ingham, Number 10's influence grew a great deal, but even Sir Bernard never achieved the power of a Michael Deaver. He certainly never exercised the iron control over Thatcher's schedule which Deaver did over Reagan's. If Michael Shea, former press secretary to the Queen, is right and proximity to power is a sure sign of influence, then Deaver was the most influential White House aide of all: his office opened directly onto the Oval Office. Poor Sir Bernard was a corridor away from Mrs Thatcher.

Sir Bernard, unlike Michael Deaver, was also concerned with influencing the newspaper correspondents rather than the TV networks. He was no doubt a believer, like Peter Mandelson, Labour's ex-Director of Communications, that broadcasters in Britain primarily set their agenda from what they read in the papers.

This is not to say that Sir Bernard was indifferent to television; on the contrary he was aware of its importance, particularly on the coverage of Prime Ministerial foreign trips. Such excursions have always been an important part of Prime Ministerial propaganda, often organized close to elections in order to portray the incumbent as a 'statesman' and to differentiate the Prime Minister from the powerless Leader of the Opposition.

Sir Bernard, who worked for a Prime Minister who raised the foreign trip to a propaganda art form, sought to achieve maximum exposure for his leader, often by the simple expedient of bullying. In a famous row with Alan Protheroe, the then Assistant Director General of the BBC, Sir Bernard bluntly hectored and threatened the Corporation to ensure they made available to ITN 'pool' pictures of Mrs Thatcher visiting the Falklands. This was to ensure that the triumphant visuals had as wide a distribution as possible.

Nor has it been beneath the dignity of a British Prime Minister to use a visual prop for dramatic TV news impact. Probably the most famous was the enormous Russian-style white fur hat that Harold Macmillan wore when he arrived at Moscow Airport in the late fifties. Mrs Thatcher was also well aware that on television news the image shouts louder than the word. On her visit to Northern Ireland, for example, immediately after the assassination by the IRA of Lord Mountbatten, she wore the red beret and flak jacket of the Parachute Regiment during her meeting with them at Crossmaglen. In such circumstances it was hardly necessary for her to voice her support for the security services: the image said it all.

Whilst Mrs Thatcher managed to portray herself to her advantage on her foreign trips, often appearing more like the monarch than the Queen, she was not so successful in the visuals she appeared in at home. The question is, in a sense, academic, since she won every General Election she fought; but her actions do reveal the lack of sophistication in the British photo-opportunity and visual when compared with the work of the master of the art, Michael Deaver. Remember: since Deaver knew that Reagan was perceived as someone who might conceivably start a war, he was always loath to have the President photographed next to any military equipment. Not so with Mrs Thatcher. Amongst the myriad of military photo-opportunities she gave was one in which she was shown actually commanding a tank. The image was an extraordinarily powerful one with Mrs Thatcher looming out from the turret of a gigantic instrument of destruction, barking commands down to her crew. The television news pictures were sent all over the world, and confirmed in the eyes of many that she was a one-dimensional 'tough guy' politician. It was, of course, a great temptation for her propagandists to play up to her strengths via the news visual, but it can be a mistake if all the propagandist is doing is reinforcing a view that people already hold about the candidate and which many voters find is a negative. Of course, it would be absurd to fly too much in the other direction. Shots of Mrs Thatcher wandering around under Waterloo Bridge giving solace to down-and-outs would be as bad a piece of dissonance as the picture of Michael Dukakis driving his tank. The solution is for the propagandist to press as far as he can in the area where the candidate is perceived to be weak *without* creating dissonance. This is always a matter of fine judgement. With Thatcher this might have been achieved by showing her with disabled people or with charities – shots to illustrate how caring she could be as an individual.

Mrs Thatcher may have occasionally appeared in visuals which were not to her best political advantage, but she never suffered the sort of visual rejection which Neil Kinnock experienced as leader of the Labour party when he travelled to the White House to meet Ronald Reagan in 1987. The President's propagandists simply decided not to allow the news crews in to record the meeting. Deaver was no longer at the White House when Reagan and Kinnock met, but the thinking behind the refusal is pure Deaver Rules. It shows that it is not the meeting itself that Reagan's staff objected to – simply the legitimacy given to the meeting by television pictures. In fact it might not be overstating the case to say that under the Deaver Rules, without television, to all intents and purposes there *was* no meeting.

As a country Britain came late to the staged visual or photo-opportunity. It wasn't until 1979, after Sir Gordon Reece had made a study of the 1976 Presidential campaign between Carter and Ford and the 1978 Congressional elections, that the Tories began the first really concerted effort to create visuals for the British TV news.

The Opposition did little in response. The 1983 Labour campaign was almost a textbook example of how not to conduct a propaganda campaign on television. The then leader, Michael Foot, scorned American-born techniques like the use of the visual, and his campaign made few allowances for television. It relied instead on the outdated technique of the 'stump' speech and senior party figures meeting voters at large rallies all over the country.

It was against the background of the Foot disaster of 1983 that Peter Mandelson became Director of Communications of the Labour party. He certainly did not scorn the visual, and a whole new visual identity was created for the party. One of the partners of corporate identity consultants Wolff Olins, Michael Wolff, designed the red rose that was to be at the heart of the gentler, more sophisticated image Mandelson wanted the Labour party to project.[7] Labour's campaign during the 1987 election was keenly stage-managed by Mandelson. He ensured that the news media were treated with an abundance of visuals and that senior party figures organized their schedules around television rather than rallies. But Mandelson is adamant that this was less than half his job. In his opinion, the fact that Labour lost the 1987 election, despite excellent propaganda techniques, shows that without policies wanted by the voter there is nothing that even the finest image-making can do. The best visuals, the cleverest manipulation of the news media, will all come to nothing if you do not deliver what the voter wants in terms of real, solid policy.

The General Election of April 1992 saw Peter Mandelson elected to Parliament as Member for Hartlepool. It also saw the Labour party lose after its leadership believed they had finally done enough to be elected on the grounds of good, solid policy. One of the many ironies of the campaign was that the Labour party, under the campaign direction of Dave Hill, produced an even finer apparent visual campaign than they had in 1987 – the year when it was said that Labour 'won the campaign but lost the election'. Similar sentiments were expressed in the press in 1992. But they were mistaken. There are occasions when glitz and glamour are inappropriate, and this was one of them. We have already discussed the dangerous messages that the Labour rally at Sheffield sent out to the voters and similar, though less overt, messages were sent out by many of the other pictures that the Labour campaign produced. Partly through an apparent desire to shield Kinnock from the tabloids and partly to dispel doubts in the voter's mind that he was Prime Ministerial material, the visual representations of Neil Kinnock did not show him to be striving to become elected. There was no Labour equivalent of the pictures of Mr Major on his soap box. It was significant that Neil Kinnock was not shown dodging insults or eggs on his campaign trail. Instead he appeared almost smug in a series of controlled photo-opportunities. It all looked too easy for him. Moreover, it looked like he was taking the election result for granted. As John Underwood, a former Labour director of Communication, said after the campaign, part of the problem was that Labour appeared too slick alongside the Conservative operation. Underwood believed that Labour should have geared their campaign in the direction that the Tory campaign developed – by implication dropping the glitzy moments and getting Neil Kinnock out onto the street, hopefully to face a hostile crowd. A few eggs thrown at his suit would not have hurt his image.

By contrast the Conservative campaign benefited from a central theme, John Major, but many of the visuals within this looked exactly as if they had been directed by a former TV producer of *That's Life* – which they had been. One of the archetypal *That's Life* visuals was the painted steam-roller that Woodward employed to smash through wooden boxes representing Labour policy, and there were the 'majorettes' who, dressed in T shirts emblazoned with the slogan 'JM 4 PM', greeted John Major and his wife on one visit to Smith Square – at least John Major had the good grace to look embarrassed.

At its worst the Tory campaign was visually embarrassing. John Major was sent to campaign at a robotics factory – not the most flattering conjunction of images for a Prime Minister not known for his charisma, and the Labour party's phone number was given at the end of one Conservative election broadcast with viewers childishly asked to phone in and complain about their policies. Indeed it's salutary to note that the idea for the strongest visual image which drew out previously unrealized qualities from the Prime Minister, the soap box, came from John Major himself.

The 1992 British Election campaign showed how the creation of the visual TV event had begun to play an increasingly important part in election strategy. But the necessity for good visuals is infinitely more important for American campaigns which do not have the coverage provided by national newspapers or lengthy national news programmes which can expose the lack of substance of each pseudo-event created by the propagandists. Compared to the dream Deaver year of 1984 the 1992 General Election demonstrated that Britain was still visually in the Dark Ages.

Notes

1. Hertsgaard, Mark: *On Bended Knee – The Press and the Reagan Presidency*

2. Deaver, Michael K., with Micky Herskowitz: *Behind the Scenes*

3. Adatto, Kiku: *Sound Bite Democracy: Network Evening News Presidential Campaign Coverage 1968 and 1988*

4. Graham, Fred: *Happy Talk*

5. From a seminar at the Barone Center for Press, Politics and Public Policy, John F. Kennedy School of Government, Harvard University

6. Noonan, Peggy: *What I Saw at the Revolution*

7. Hughes, Colin, and Patrick Wintour: *Labour Rebuilt*

Chapter Six

Interviews and Debates

The propagandist strives for control. But there will be occasions when the propagandist, like even the most protective parent, must let his charge out of his care. At some point in an election the candidate will have to respond himself to the questions of a journalist or the attacks of his opponent. These are the dangerous times for today's TV propagandist, especially when there is chance that a dissonance will appear between the carefully structured image of the candidate created by the 'paid' media in the adverts, and the stumbling or diffident performance that a candidate might give in an interview or debate. The propagandist must devote time, effort and money to coaching his candidate on how to answer questions and how to debate on television.

The man in the arena

Roger Ailes first entered the consultancy business in 1968 when he was asked to produce Richard Nixon in a new debate concept of great cleverness. The premise was straightforward: since what the viewer enjoys in a debate is the sense that the candidate is exposed, raw and under threat, why not create that sensation but in a way that is controlled by the propagandist? A series of ten programmes were proposed by the Nixon team, each of which would show Nixon facing a different selection of interrogators who would each ask him questions, live, in front of a studio audience. Nixon would stand in the centre of the set, prowling around as if under attack, creating the impression that he was defending himself against unpredictable forces and seeing them off entirely on his own.

Whilst the Nixon team chose the questioners they were careful to include some critics of Nixon's and, taken in isolation, some of the questions that Nixon faced were as tough as any he answered from journalists at a press conference. But it is important to realize the televisual differences between a press conference and the controlled Nixon debates produced by Ailes. The television concept of 'The Man in the Arena' (as the format came to be known) was to create the maximum impression of danger whilst minimizing the risk. A questioner asking a tough question in the Nixon studio, in front of a pro-Nixon crowd, faced a much harder time than a journalist asking questions at a press conference where the candidate might genuinely be put on the defensive.

Even if a tough question was thrown at Nixon as the 'Man in the Arena', a merely adequate response would receive rapturous applause. And the format allowed him one other crucial advantage. The only way to get to the heart of an issue in a television interview is by detailed, progressive questioning, one question following on another. In the 'Man in the Arena' format, each interrogator was allowed just one question and one supplementary, so it was impossible to conduct a coherent investigation of anything. The answers could be as superficial and evasive as Nixon chose. And here's the wonderful news for the propagandist: the irony is that this format, which guarantees that the candidate cannot be pressed on any issue, carries with it on television the impression that the candidate is in more danger than if he was simply sitting in a studio and answering detailed questions from a single interrogator.

Interview rules

'The Man in the Arena' is the propagandist's dream format. The candidate is protected, yet the television viewer perceives him as

144

vulnerable. But what if the candidate cannot be protected? After all, the Nixon campaign paid for the 'Man in the Arena' programmes and most campaigns would baulk at paying for debate time. No, the propagandist must face the uncomfortable truth that his candidate is going to have to be exposed to potentially hostile questions on television, which is why the politician must first be taught how to conduct himself.

The majority of the consultants whom I talked to agreed on the basic interview rules which every candidate should follow. Chief amongst them is never to appear on a documentary-type programme that has to be edited. As Roger Ailes wrote in *You Are the Message*, 'The truth is that they will be interviewed for two hours and the Network will use their most controversial eighteen seconds.' Of course, the news itself is edited, but that is different, for if the candidate is dealing with a news reporter, he knows that only one or two brief extracts from his answers are liable to be used; in addition he is familiar with the format of the news report. A documentary, on the other hand, is both longer and more complex in realization and much less within the control or understanding of the candidate. So the propagandist is wise to define the circumstances of the candidate's participation. In essence the only situation in which the aware propagandist will ideally allow his candidate to be interviewed is a live (or recorded 'as live') show, where he knows in advance from the producers both the question areas that are to be covered and the name and professional style of the interviewer.

The most memorable American example in recent years of just how interview coaching and an awareness of the strengths and weaknesses of the medium of television turned around the perception of a candidate was the confrontation between George Bush and Dan Rather on CBS News in 1988. Roger Ailes, George Bush's political consultant, first insisted that CBS do the interview live. The interview was conducted 'down the line' – that is, with Rather in the CBS News studios in New York and Bush in his office in the Capitol. Rather was trying to quiz Bush in detail about his role during the Arms for Hostages controversy. Unknown to TV viewers, Ailes was just feet away from Bush throughout the interview.[1] Bush was replying aggressively, aided by Ailes who was holding up key words on a yellow pad to let Bush know what to say. Bush turned the tables on Rather in one dramatic moment by saying, 'It's not fair to judge my whole career by a rehash on Iran. How would you like it if I judged your whole career by those seven minutes when you walked off the set in New York?' This was a reference to the occasion when Rather had refused to come on to the set because the starting time of the CBS evening news had been delayed by a previous programme which was over-running. For a moment Rather looked nonplussed under Bush's counter-attack, but then he pressed on with the interview. To the average viewer the contest looked exciting and emotional, though in terms of *information* the interview contained nothing new – but since this was television that was hardly the point.

Ailes wanted Bush to respond aggressively for a number of important reasons. First, Bush gave the impression that he was the one being bullied, and therefore the viewer was likely to sympathize with him. Second, Ailes was conscious that, despite a heroic, even John Wayne-ish war record, Bush was perceived in some quarters of the media as a wimp, so an aggressive performance against Rather would help banish that impression. Third, one of the most valuable techniques a candidate can use when confronted by an aggressive interviewer is to turn the question back on the questioner. This can be extremely effective, as it was in this case, because it breaks the unwritten rule that you don't question the interviewer. Almost always it puts the interviewer off his stride.

Ailes and his staff have even worked out a formula which candidates can use to answer questions. The formula is $Q = A + 1$,[2] which simply means that if the candidate is asked a question (Q) he should answer it briefly (A) before adding on any key points from his own 'agenda' (+ 1). So, to take an example from Chapter 4, if the then Mayor of Denver had been asked, 'Why are you spending taxpayers' money on six bodyguards? [Q]' he should answer: 'Because the Chief of Police thought that number was necessary for my protection after death threats had been received against me [A]. As Mayor I think it vital that we do everything we can to uphold the rule of law in this city. All citizens should be able to walk the streets in safety [+ 1].'

Another technique – one that is surprisingly successful – is for the candidate occasionally to admit that he has made a mistake. In *You Are the Message* Ailes quotes the example of Ed Koch, an ex-mayor of New York, who was questioned about the failure of his plan to install cycle lanes in Manhattan. In answer to the first question in a half-hour programme devoted to the subject, Koch said, 'You're right, it was a terrible idea.' That was effectively the end of the programme. All the reporter could do was to keep saying, 'It was a terrible idea, wasn't it?' to which Koch would say, 'Yes, that's what I just said.' In Britain recently, Lord King, Chairman of British Airways and a master of the television interview, went on the news to admit that mistakes had been made during an anti-terrorist exercise involving the use of one of BA's planes. As Chairman he took full responsibility for what had happened. This effectively defused the story. In America, as in Britain, it is recognized that television news acts best when there is controversy. A story can never have 'legs' if someone admits they were at fault. Of course, this technique must be sparingly used, or the candidate will look incompetent. It works best when the person admitting fault is perceived as a tough, no-nonsense guy, like Lord King or Ed Koch.

Another important technique is to teach the candidate to 'come in under' the tone of the interviewer – the candidate should listen not merely to what the interviewer is saying, but also to the tone in which he is saying it. If the tone of the interviewer's voice becomes more aggressive, then the candidate's voice should become calmer. This makes the candidate look in control of his emotions whilst the interviewer does not.

Preparing for an interview is vital. One bad interview can destroy a campaign; it can almost destroy a career. Edward Kennedy's interview with Roger Mudd in 1983, in which the Senator could not even provide a coherent response to the question, 'Why do you want to be President?' marked the end of his challenge against Jimmy Carter.

The visual nature of television means there are those who believe that what the candidates actually *say* during interviews is not the most important way they communicate. Glen Berlin, President of Berlin Training and Development, makes a good living out of teaching candidates how to perfect their non-verbal communication. 'Up to 90 per cent of communication is non-verbal,' he told me, 'and candidates ignore this at their peril.' Berlin, who first became interested in non-verbal communication as a method for picking up women, believes that 'If a candidate's message is subliminally interpreted in a way different from the overt, spoken message, that candidate is failing at his primary task of persuasion. A potential big money contributor, for example, may be meeting a candidate for the first time. Based upon the non-verbal messages sent by the candidate the contributor develops a feeling that he does not really mean what he says. As a result of these feelings the potential donor may stay on the sideline and keep his wallet shut.'[3]

Berlin teaches candidates a variety of ways in which they should stand, sit and gesture. Standing upright with your hands clasped loosely in front of you – in a pose known as the 'fig leaf' – shows you're defensive. Do you have a habit of jabbing your finger forward to make a point? Forget it, you're probably coming across as too aggressive. Do you stand with your hands in your pockets in the mistaken belief that it makes you look relaxed? Wrong. It makes you look closed off to the other person's argument. Do you stand with your hands in your pockets *and* jiggle loose change about whilst trying to solicit money from a potential campaign sponsor? This is a common situation on Berlin's course. Stop it – you'll put your sugar-daddy off completely.

Berlin teaches his clients the need to respect 'an individual's spatial needs'. He reveals that there are four distinct zones of space: intimate, social, personal and public. He advises his clients to try and remain in the 'personal' zone (from eighteen inches to four feet away) while conducting campaign business. He says: 'Unfortunately, some candidates insist on intruding into the voter's intimate zone [closer than eighteen inches], thereby causing feelings of discomfort and alienation.' It turns out that 'the most common dilemma is the handshake. Too often politicians insist on utilizing what are called "handshake enhancers". Grasping a wrist, forearm, elbow or shoulders are all forms of handshake enhancers and force the person whose hand is being shaken to be in closer proximity for longer periods of time, causing him physical discomfort.'

Non-verbal communication is no minor matter in the television age. Berlin states unequivocally that 'smart candidates will make sure that their non-verbal messages are congruent with the verbal messages, thereby dramatically increasing the probability of being understood, believed and elected'.[4]

It is easy for the sophisticated journalist or academic to scoff at Berlin's work. At first glance it seems inconsequential; almost, in some cynical eyes, the equivalent of employing an astrologer or, at the least, a masseur for the candidate's ego. But to think this way is a mistake. American political consultants can be criticized on a number of levels, but no one can say they throw their candidate's money around. Everyone involved in the election process recognizes the importance of money – it is the one subject that no one jokes about. Glen Berlin and his non-verbal tuition classes are booked because the candidates and their consultants believe they work. And in this business the test of whether they work is simple – they help get the candidate elected.

Debates

The American TV consultant is even more wary of televised debates than of the formal television interview. The medium of television conspires to reduce these debates to the point where all that is left are key 'defining moments' – code for moments where one of the candidates puts down his opponent or is put down himself. Such 'defining moments' live much longer than the debates themselves. One such moment was when, during his debate with Jimmy Carter, Gerald Ford inadvertently said Poland was not under Soviet domination: Another was the exchange between Lloyd Bentsen and Dan Quayle, culminating in Bentsen's exquisite put-down of Quayle's attempt to compare himself with Kennedy. 'Senator, I knew Jack Kennedy. Jack Kennedy was a friend of mine. Senator, you're no Jack Kennedy.' The television image of Quayle with his 'rabbit trapped in the oncoming glare of the headlights' expression was the only image the vast majority of viewers will have taken away from the debate – all the more so since this was the 'sound bite' which the networks played over and over again afterwards. If most people relied on the printed media to make their judgement – if they were reading a report or a transcript of the debate – such a moment would not be of enormous significance. You had to see it up close for it to hit home.

Ailes himself was involved in what was probably the most

'defining moment' in any Presidential campaign. He had been asked by Michael Deaver and others from the President's staff to coach Reagan for the second of the televised debates with Walter Mondale. Reagan had given a poor performance in the first debate, stumbling and unsure. He had been coached by his staff to try and provide detail in his answers. Details were never Reagan's strong point. Ailes writes that he said to the President, 'You didn't get elected on details, you got elected on themes. Every time a question is asked, relate it to one of your themes.' This, as we have seen, is classic TV propaganda advice. But Ailes did more than simply give this advice. He warned the President that the toughest question he faced was going to be on the 'age issue'. Ailes sensed that the American public wanted to vote Reagan back into office, but they wanted reassurance that he wasn't too old for the job. Ailes told the President what no one else had dared – that he should deal with the 'age issue' head-on.

That advice meant that when the subject was referred to in the debate Ailes knew the President could deal with it. Reagan's response was: 'I want you to know that I will not make age an issue of this campaign. I am not going to exploit for political purposes my opponent's youth and inexperience.' Reagan brought the house down. Even Mondale smiled. There is no better example of how humour on television can deflect the audience's attention away from a serious issue. For the issue of Reagan's age, and thus his fitness to govern, should have been a major issue of the campaign, yet it was successfully deflated by a joke. Is this a suitable way of answering the public's concern? It is impossible to imagine such a response working on any other medium except television. Professor Postman has written eloquently about the famous Lincoln–Douglas debates in the nineteenth century during which each candidate would talk for three hours and then have one hour to rebut. But as the Professor told me, 'Television says, "No, here's what we'll do. We'll have Bush and Dukakis stand there and someone will ask Bush, 'Mr Vice-President, what do you think is the cause of the trouble in the Middle East and the solution to the problem? You have two minutes to answer – after which Governor Dukakis will have one minute for rebuttal.'" Now one could say that Bush should at that point turn to the interlocutor and say, "how dare you ask such a question and give me two minutes to reply and Governor Dukakis one minute for rebuttal? What sort of men do you think we are?" Or at the very least say, "How dare you ask such a question? What sort of electorate do you think we are?"'

The fact that the debates are on television is the key to understanding the way the propagandist approaches them. Brevity of response is the first quality called for. Abraham Lincoln would have failed badly. Hubert Humphrey was thought inept when he gave an eleven-minute response to one question on his 1968 election eve television debate. Brevity is seen as competence – something which, as Professor Postman points out, is extraordinary as a judgement of a candidate's approach to complex issues. Second, the candidate's physical appearance becomes of crucial importance. Michael Deaver recounts with ill-concealed glee how he was allowed to dictate the way the lights would look in one of the Reagan–Mondale debates. As a result he installed plenty of 'top' lighting. 'Mondale had gotten this big make-up artist from Hollywood so what he wanted was head-on lighting and lots of it. But the top lighting meant he had huge circles under his eyes. The Mondale people didn't have any lighting people with them. They didn't understand how important it was.'[5] Such is the stuff of Presidential politics today.

The British experience

Interview technique is one area where the British politician is at least as sophisticated as his or her American counterpart. For reasons already examined, British political candidates have to deal more frequently than their American cousins with television journalists throwing unscripted questions. It was not always this way. In the early days of the BBC, questions were actually scripted and submitted to the politician in advance, but the advent of Independent Television News in 1961 changed this cosy arrangement. Nowadays an essential prerequisite for any British politician's success is the ability to deal spontaneously with difficult questions posed by a range of TV interviewers.

British politicians have had to develop television techniques to deal with questions ranging from the banal to the brutal. The first to show complete mastery of the interview was Harold Wilson, who was an artist at disconcerting the interviewer. Whenever Wilson needed time to think he would pause and light his pipe, something which had the effect on television of distracting the audience's attention away from the subject under discussion. Gerald Kaufman, who was Harold Wilson's parliamentary press officer for five years in the late sixties, reveals Wilson's technique for interviews: 'He didn't go to the studio to answer questions: the questions were an irrelevance which had to be listened to. He went there to say something. He decided what he wanted to say – the message he wanted to communicate to the people who were watching and then, regardless of the questions that were put to him, he said what he meant to say.'[6] This, of course, is a technique favoured by many politicians. The cleverest among them have a set phrase which enables them to move into their prepared statement as if they were actually answering the question. Such phrases include: 'The best way I can answer that is to let you know just what my position is on . . .' or 'I think that's an important point, but almost more important is . . .'. Anyone who has conducted television interviews knows that it is next to impossible to interview a politician who simply does not wish to co-operate. I once interviewed a Foreign Office minister who expertly gave convincing answers to questions I had not asked. On studying the transcript of the interview I saw that he had been prefacing most answers with the phrase, 'Let me tell you why I disagree with that . . .' or 'You can't phrase the question in those terms because . . .'. The television interviewer is much more vulnerable to this expert evasion than the viewer realizes – a fact which, of course, helps the politician.

The ways in which Neil Kinnock, Margaret Thatcher and John Major answer (or evade) questions during TV interviews has even been the subject of an academic study, conducted by York University lecturer Peter Bull and his colleague Kate Mayer. They discovered that at least half the time each of these three senior politicians did not answer the question posed to them. But the techniques used by each were markedly different. John Major often used what one might term the 'Ed Koch' approach and simply admitted that he did not know the answer or was not prepared to give it. The benefit of this technique is that the candidate appears straightforward and honest; the disadvantage is that he might also come over as ignorant or naive. Mrs Thatcher evaded questions by the blunderbuss technique. She simply turned on the interviewer. Advantage: the candidate comes across as decisive. Disadvantage: the candidate might look like a bully. Neil Kinnock used a mixture of these two techniques plus one of his own devising: he simply talked for longer (74 per cent of the interview, compared with 64.5 per cent for John Major). Advantage of this technique: you can appear erudite. Disadvantage: you look like a windbag. Different politicians, different techniques of evading the questions, with all three politicians having one thing in common. For half the time they did not answer the questions put to them.

British politicians do not seem as aware as their American counterparts that the TV interview is decided as much by the personality of the questioner as the content of the question. It was no accident that the only time Mrs Thatcher was ever really threatened during a TV interview was by an 'ordinary' viewer who on *Nationwide* in 1983 asked her about the reasoning behind the sinking of the Argentinian warship *General Belgrano* during the Falklands War. Mrs Thatcher tried her usual trick of rounding on the interviewer, but because in this case her interrogator was a housewife, unsophisticated in the unwritten conventions of such encounters, she did not realize that the interviewer is supposed to sit back and take the criticism. So the housewife responded to Mrs Thatcher's unreasonable attack with an unreasonable attack of her own. Anyone who has seen the tape of this confrontation realizes that, paradoxically, it was the very amateurishness of the questioner that broke through Mrs Thatcher's carapace of protection. An amateur, who is by definition the underdog, seems to have a better chance of unsettling the politician than does the professional. Indeed, not just amateurs but adolescent amateurs, featured on a discussion programme called *Open to Question* made by BBC Scotland, have shown themselves to be extremely effective at cross-examining politicians.

Comedians also present problems for the politician. One of the most effective pieces of propaganda advice Neil Kinnock ever received was from comedian Stephen Fry, who wrote in his column in the *Listener* that Kinnock should concentrate on making Mrs Thatcher appear a figure of fun. Another comedian, Clive Anderson

– who, unusually, is also a qualified barrister – has also proved skilled at unsettling politicians. He interviewed Dave Nellist, the controversial Labour MP for Coventry East. When Nellist used one of the tactics discussed above and did not answer the question, Anderson spoke simply and honestly in a way no experienced current affairs interviewer would. He said: 'I'm not used to interviewing politicians, so I'm still waiting for an answer to my previous question.' And when interviewing Tony Benn MP, who was similarly evading a question by simply switching to another subject, Anderson interrupted: 'Complete this sentence; arguing by false analogy is like . . .' Benn, one of the toughest and most experienced of television performers, was nonplussed. All this shows why an experienced propagandist is careful to ensure not just that the interview with his candidate is conducted live (or as live), but that he knows the tactics and techniques of the interviewer. 'Never let your candidate appear with a comedian' ought to be the maxim engraved on every propagandist's heart.

There are tactics the television producer can use which give the propagandist little room for manoeuvre. The most difficult to deal with is the single example. It is hard to debate government policy on homelessness with a homeless mother and her three children. The medium of television naturally highlights the human drama at the expense of the broad statistic. On *Man Alive*, a BBC social affairs programme, some years ago, a senior policeman who advocated the 'have a go' policy, in which members of the public were advised to fight back against intruders, was confronted by a studio audience of maimed and disfigured guests. All of them had suffered as a result of 'having a go'. From the first moment of the debate the policeman had lost: the sympathy of the audience was with the victims.

The most common debate format that a television producer will try to create is the adversarial one, in which the argument is between two totally opposing points of view. The producers will often approach politicians at either end of a controversy rather than those in the middle, because argument televises well. It also gives the appearance that the interviewer is impartial – an umpire between two polarized points of view. This method was neatly encapsulated by a presenter of BBC *Nationwide* at the end of just such a studio argument, 'So,' he said in his closing remarks. 'One says yes, and one says no. It's up to you at home to decide.' One tactic (a parallel to the blunt acceptance of responsibility) for derailing the producer's planned argument is for the politician to agree with much of what his opponent is saying. This effectively stops the debate and makes the politician concerned look reasonable.

How the candidate dresses for the interview is also important. Labour party communications officials made certain that front-benchers could take advantage of the personal presentation advice offered by Barbara Follett, who gives advice on hairstyle, dress and make-up.[7] The essence of such advice is that the candidate's dress should project an image in sympathy with the broad character impression the candidate wants to put before the voter. A man is perceived differently on TV if he wears a serious blue suit or a sports jacket, a woman if she wears a shoulder padded jacket or a floral dress. Again, those who scoff at the importance of such advice should remember the public outcry that greeted the appearance of Michael Foot in a duffle coat on Remembrance Day. The then Labour leader was wearing a perfectly clean and pressed item of clothing, but because it had connotations with casual wear he was castigated in the popular press. Why? Because at home the millions watching him on television were making judgements about his fitness to govern based on the type of coat he was wearing.

Immediately after Saddam Hussein's invasion of Kuwait, President Bush was careful what clothing messages he gave out during his press conferences at his holiday home at Kennebunkport in Maine. In few news reports of the period will you find the President wearing his working uniform of blue suit and tie. This was not some oversight on his part. The wearing of a formal suit would send the signal that he was working; his propagandists created the impression that the President was on holiday but still in touch with events. They remembered the negative impression created when President Carter appeared to be trapped in the White House at the time of the Iranian hostage crisis.

So the propagandist should ensure that his candidate is dressed correctly for the interview, has the right body language signals at his disposal, will stay calm and 'come in under' the tone of the questioner, is armed with the key points he wants to make, and is prepared to make them regardless of what the interviewer says.

What more could the propagandist possibly do to ensure his candidate's success? As will be seen in Chapter 7, the logic of today's television propaganda dictates that he should not just try and get his candidate to be a guest *on* a chat show; he should try to get his candidate to *host* a chat show.

Notes

1. Taylor, Paul: *See How They Run – Electing the President in an Age of Mediaocracy*

2. Ailes, Roger: *You Are the Message*

3. *Campaigns and Elections* magazine, December 1991

4. Ibid

5. Deaver, Michael K., with Micky Herskowitz: *Behind the Scenes*

6. Cockerell, Michael: *Live from Number 10*

7. Hughes, Colin, and Patrick Wintour: *Labour Rebuilt*

Chapter Seven

The Way Ahead

Anyone interested in the future of television propaganda would do well to study the experience of the Romanians who lived under Nicolae Ceausescu. Not for the obvious reasons that spring to the informed mind: the memory of the pivotal role that television played in the brief and bloody revolution at the end of 1989; the recollection of the dramatic pictures beamed from Romanian TV studios in Bucharest. No, the Romanian experience rewards study in this context because it is one of the clearest examples of how Goebbels's great truth still lives – entertainment is the best form of propaganda. For when Ceausescu stopped entertaining, his reign was as good as over.

A Romanian soap opera

If you travel to Bucharest and then drive out into the countryside through the bleak and featureless landscape, past the half-bulldozed villages and the gypsy huts, stop in any hamlet and talk to any peasant in any field and ask them what TV programmes they liked during Ceausescu's rule, they will as likely as not answer with one word – *Dallas*. For the soap opera about the Ewings was an enormous hit in Ceausescu's Romania, along with other imported

American series like *Columbo, Kojak* and *The Streets of San Francisco*. Even more extraordinary, for a British visitor, is the fact that many of the peasants will tell you how they were crazy for *The Onedin Line*, a BBC Television drama series about the adventures of a nineteenth-century shipowner. 'I really felt for Captain Onedin,' a gnarled farm worker told me. 'He had such terrible problems with his ships.' Western entertainment programmes like *The Onedin Line* had a profound effect on Romanian life. Vlad Ihora was ten at the time, living with his parents in a small, three-room apartment in Bucharest. He remembers that *The Onedin Line* was shown 'every Sunday. At five o'clock everyone was in front of the TV with a coffee or a tea and we were watching *The Onedin Line*. People used to say, "Don't call me on the phone now, I'm busy."'

This came about because Ceausescu disliked his Communist neighbours and wanted better relations with the West. He even went on a state visit to Britain in 1979 and stayed with the Queen in Buckingham Palace. As an unforeseen consequence of this rapprochement Western countries like Britain and America offered to sell Ceausescu their TV programmes (this, whilst the oppression in Romania was amongst the worst of any Communist regime). The TV material was cheap, and since Ceausescu did not think that entertainment drama was in any way a Western propaganda tool, he agreed to show the programmes.

Many ordinary Romanians told me how the foreign soap operas were their most important, often their only source of entertainment amidst the terrible drabness of Ceausescu's Romania. As Goebbels discovered in the bleak days after Stalingrad, few if any of the audience make a link between the glamorous lifestyle shown on the screen – oozing capitalist values and conspicuous expenditure – and the deprivation they are suffering themselves. Like the Germans who watched the exotic *Baron Munchausen* while they were living from hand to mouth and being bombed, the Romanians looked on *Dallas* as an escapist fantasy. It could as easily have been about Martians as about life elsewhere on the planet. In any case, the ordinary Romanian was as likely to go to Mars as to Texas.

Then, all of a sudden, in the early 1980s, a disaster occurred. '*Dallas* just stopped suddenly,' says Mrs Ihora, Vlad's mother. 'We never found out what happened.' The Romanians had to wait until the end of the decade before they finally found out who shot JR. No one knows for certain why Ceausescu stopped the foreign TV shows. There had never really been an ideological motive for showing them in the first place; they had simply been a cheap way of filling up airtime and had grown more and more popular. One possibility is that the shows were stopped as part of the overall austerity measures that Ceausescu introduced. For television this meant that transmission hours were cut to only two hours a night. Mrs Felitia Melascanu, who worked for Romanian TV before the revolution, explained: 'We were told that the Ceausescu family – Ceausescu and his wife – were able to watch only two hours of television a day and they wanted to watch all of the programmes.' And what the Ceausescu family liked to watch of an evening was film of the Ceausescu family. So most of the two hours was taken up with film of what the Ceausescus had done that day or news of what they would do tomorrow. The programmes were unwatchably dull – for anyone other than the Ceausescu family. And after Ceausescu had paid a visit to fellow megalomaniac President Kim of North Korea, they became even duller – a feat many had thought impossible. In Korea Ceausescu had seen even more inept TV propaganda, featuring endless films of parades held in honour of President Kim. But Ceausescu loved programmes like this and broadcast some of them on Romanian TV.

Ceausescu clearly never thought of the consequences of reducing Romanian TV to a private, in-house home-movie channel for the Ceausescu family. He made a mistake common to many megalomaniacs, thinking that in his police state people could be forced to watch his soporific propaganda. It was a mistake that Goebbels would never have been guilty of, and it is a mistake that was at least partly responsible for costing Ceausescu his life.

The Romanians who had looked forward to *Dallas* and *The Onedin Line* as the high spots of their colourless lives were distraught. What could they do? Well, first they could scale the roofs of their apartment blocks, twiddle their aerials and see what else they could receive. They discovered that with just a little alteration (or a new aerial) they could receive Bulgarian TV. Although Bulgarian TV was transmitting from a Communist state at least it was broadcast more than two hours a night. It also had one huge advantage over Romanian TV – it didn't feature Nicolae Ceausescu.

Gradually, a forest of new aerials sprouted over Bucharest and other Romanian cities. The aerials which were best for picking up Bulgarian TV were circular and easily distinguishable from the normal Romanian kind. So why didn't the Securitate tear them all down and prosecute those who dared to receive programmes from beyond the borders of this closed, secretive country – a country where every citizen who spoke so much as one word to a non-Romanian had to go to the police station and fill out a report? Like so many questions about pre-revolution life in Romania, no one knows the answer. But it seems likely that the Securitate did nothing for a number of reasons. No one thought Bulgarian TV posed any sort of threat to the regime. The aerials started appearing gradually. And, probably most important of all, members of the Securitate were almost certainly as bored with Ceausescu's TV as the rest of the population and just as anxious as the next man to be able to watch Bulgarian football matches.

Professor Pavel Campeanu of Bucharest University has studied the way in which the television viewers of Romania made their silent protest. He believes that 'the Romanian way of surviving under Ceausescu's dictatorship was a feigned obedience. You didn't obey but you didn't protest. But this change of TV was the first public protest, and the form of the protest was the operation on the roofs of special antennas allowing us in Bucharest, for instance, to watch Bulgarian TV. Because the antennas were on the roof this was public. This was a public answer saying these people are not happy with the over-ideologized programme of the official TV and this population want something different.' And along with this silent and obvious protest came an added benefit. The people who had chosen to take this risk and watch Bulgarian TV had been motivated by their desire for entertainment. But as an unforeseen consequence they were able to see other programmes as well – particularly current affairs and news. Bulgaria was at that time a Communist country, to be sure, but its news service was nothing like as crudely propagandized as Romania's. So, gradually, the population became a little more informed about the rest of the world; it began to see the world without the censoring lens of Ceausescu's TV.

The second way the population protested against the removal of entertainment programmes was by buying video recorders. Even though, at that time, a video recorder cost as much as a car, given the choice many people still preferred the video. A trade grew in smuggled video cassettes – and what did most people choose to watch? Why, Hollywood blockbusters, of course, films like *Die Hard*, or Steve Martin comedies. Again, the Securitate not only did nothing to prevent this trade in videotapes – some of them became involved in it themselves. One can almost imagine them thinking: 'What harm can it possibly do if our people watch illicit Steve Martin comedies?' Clearly, none of them had studied Goebbels. For the Reichsminister would have realized at once that in the depressed atmosphere of Ceausescu's Romania one of the most potent forms of propaganda would be entertainment drama which contained *no* overt propagandist message. Once an environment was created in which even members of the security forces felt they had to 'bend' the law in the search for entertainment, then the fabric of the disciplined state had begun to fray.

The exact role that these events played in the revolution can never be measured. But we do know that it was access to Bulgarian TV that enabled many Romanian citizens to see a revolutionary momentum developing in Czechoslovakia and East Germany in the autumn of 1989 prior to the uprising in their own country. This must have made Romanians realize that they were not alone – that they could be part of a broad sweep of history.

This still leaves the intriguing question – would Ceausescu still be in power if he had not cancelled *Dallas* and *The Onedin Line*? After all, the only reason most Romanians had turned to Bulgarian TV was the cut-back in locally transmitted foreign entertainment programmes. Few, if any, were motivated by a desire to see more accurate news coverage. I put this question to Professor Steriade of Bucharest University. She replied, 'This is not a nice question. I don't want to think what would have happened if they didn't know what was happening around them. But this is true, that having all the Western programmes but not the information would have kept people quieter. But it didn't happen like that and let's say that was our luck – even if we were so sorry not to know if J.R. was dead or not!'

What consequences does all this have for the democratic propagandist? Unlike the totalitarian propagandist he cannot sit and decide which entertainment programmes are broadcast. In a democracy it can safely be left to the commercial television networks to provide entertainment-based programmes, since any advertising-funded network will naturally gravitate towards programmes that provide the biggest audience – and such programmes are almost always entertainment vehicles. But it would be an enormous mistake for the democratic propagandist to think that such a state of affairs means that he cannot use these insights for his own work. He can, and in some countries of the world he is already beginning to.

An Indian soap

Leaving aside the first lesson the propagandist can learn from the Romanian experience – that he must make sure his own propaganda is couched not in ideological but in entertainment terms – today's propagandist should examine the impact which entertainment drama has on a population, particularly a semi-literate population. Is it not incredible that ten years after the transmission of *The Onedin Line* a Romanian peasant can remember the storyline of the series? Suppose the character who played Mr Onedin could be made to endorse your candidate? Suppose your candidate got to play the actual part of Mr Onedin? An incredible idea? Not necessarily.

India has come late to television. For the last fifty years it has been a country of films, and occasionally film stars have been elected as politicians – after all, Ronald Reagan was a movie actor. But a new propaganda phenomenon has occurred as a result of the growing impact of television on Indian society.

The late Prime Minister Rajiv Gandhi initiated a policy to ensure that every village had a communal television.[1] The intention was that the villagers would gather round the set to learn about educational matters and perhaps also about current affairs from the programmes of Dordashan, the government-controlled television service. But none of these plans have come to pass. Instead of gathering to watch either the news or educational programmes, the villagers gather to watch – of course – entertainment drama.

The most successful of the recent entertainment dramas was *The Ramayan*, a seventy-eight-part soap opera based on a classic Hindu epic. The impact of the series on Indian society was unlike anything experienced before. At its peak, out of a total population of 850 million people 650 million were watching *The Ramayan* on a Sunday morning. There has never been a soap opera like it. Such was its impact that surgical operations were postponed so that doctor and patient could watch. Trains would stop in stations for the duration of the episode. When the power station in one town broke down just before transmission there was a riot, and the disappointed *Ramayan*-less crowd set fire to the generators.

The creator of *The Ramayan*, the man who wrote and produced it, is called Ramanand Sagar. He is a seventy-four-year-old ex-commercial film-maker, an extraordinary, larger than life figure. I met him on the set of his latest epic, *Krishna*, shooting hundreds of miles from Bombay to avoid the distractions of the big city. Sagar believes he was divinely inspired to make *The Ramayan*. 'When I look back at my total career of about half a century of film-making, I was working as an apprentice to learn the language of cinema because the master of all wanted me to do this work in this language.'

In casting his epic Sagar was careful that only previously unknown actors were used. 'I didn't want any person with the briefest image to play these roles,' he says. 'I wanted the actor playing Ram to be Ram, known as Ram, not known as some other name. Where we were able to succeed was that people identified with our artistes. Many people in the villages won't know their names – they only know the name of the character they played.'

At first sight *The Ramayan* appears to be an utterly apolitical piece of entertainment; but, as Goebbels knew, there is seldom such a creature. Because the subject was the ancient Hindu stories of the derring-do of the gods, the series had a unifying effect on its primarily Hindu audience. This was deliberate. It may not have been in the mind of the creator of the series, but it was certainly in the minds of the politicians whose responsibility it was to authorize the transmission of such work on the government-run TV channel. Iqbal Masood is one of India's leading television critics. Together with a few other journalists he attended a breakfast meeting with Rajiv

Gandhi in 1987. 'A number of us told him that it is a political decision you have made to put on *Ramayan,*' Masood said to me. 'We told Gandhi, "What on earth do you mean by putting it on?" So his advisers and aides told us that the charts and structural surveys show that it is very popular.' After the meeting Masood pressed his point and discovered that some people around Gandhi had a 'very distinct fear of disorder in India at that time. It had been so from the early eighties. A deliberate decision was made to go over to religion – the kind of influence which will dampen these flare-ups.'

Masood believes that Rajiv Gandhi hoped and intended that the showing of mythological epics like *The Ramayan* would result in greater support for his Congress party. But the plan backfired badly. It was the Hindu fundamentalist party, the BJP, that reaped the benefit of the series; so much so that BJP officials approached a number of actors from *The Ramayan* and asked them to stand for Parliament at the forthcoming General Election – previous political experience not necessary.

Two actors from the cast agreed to stand. Both were elected. One was the character actor Arvind Trevidi, who played the part of Rawan in the series. When I visited him in his flat in Bombay he was open and honest when I asked whether he could have been elected to Parliament if he hadn't been in *The Ramayan*. 'No, that's not possible,' he replied. Trevidi is now responsible for a constituency of 1.3 million people. But he does not want to devote his life to politics. 'I will give my first preference to my profession. Because I have earned all my bread and butter from my business of acting – not from politics.'

The aspiring propagandist might ask what's new about Mr Trevidi. Actors have got lucky before. Film stars have become MPs – even Presidents. What's new is that Mr Trevidi was a relatively unknown 'stage artiste' before appearing in *The Ramayan*. He played one character which brought him into public consciousness, and he played that same character for hour after hour. In a semi-literate country, is it not natural that some people might have voted for him because of a confusion between Trevidi and the character he played – a wily schemer, not unlike a Hindu J.R. Ewing? Trevidi accepts that this is possible, saying enigmatically, 'People express themselves in their own ways.'

Film actors most often play different characters in every film. So a confusion between the actor himself and the character he plays is unlikely. The reverse is true on television, where a serial soap can run for years. To imagine the difference between Larry Hagman and J.R. Ewing is difficult. Indeed, the publicity surrounding series like *Dallas* actively encourages such confusion. When Larry Hagman/ J.R. Ewing came to Britain at the height of the popularity of *Dallas* he appeared on TV chat shows *as* J.R. The symbiosis between actor and character was almost total. In a recent libel case in Britain an actor called William Roache, who plays Ken Barlow in *Coronation Street*, successfully sued a newspaper which had said that he was boring and smug and hated by other actors in the series. Several times during the evidence, other cast members confused themselves with their TV characters. Even Bill Roache succumbed to the odd slip of the tongue occasionally. Who can blame him? Such an actor must constantly get letters and questions directed to his TV persona, as if the character were a real person and had a life outside the television studio.

This phenomenon has reached its logical end in the person of a pretty young actress called Dipika Chikhlia. When she was twenty, in 1985, Ramanand Sagar cast her to play the role of the goddess Sita in *The Ramayan*. Sitting in her spacious Bombay flat, Dipika told me of the significance of Sita in Indian mythology. 'The very fact that you say "Sita" – ladies feel they would automatically be in heaven. So it's just one of those kinds of things – just chanting Sita's name can open the doors to heaven.' Sita is a magical figure in Indian life, particularly amongst the peasants. 'Sita's image was a very clean and pious image,' says Dipika, 'which anyone and everybody immediately took a liking to.' Dipika was told by Sagar after her audition, 'You *are* Sita.' And Dipika accepts that one of the keys to the success of the series was that because relative unknowns were used every character was played by an actor who resembled the idealized image of the character in the audience's mind. Thus to many of the viewers of *The Ramayan* Dipika *was* Sita, so much so that she told me, 'I had all kinds of fanmail coming across to me and they did treat me like Sita. I mean I still have letters where my name is Dipika and in brackets they write Sita. And even the postman knows it immediately it comes to Bombay. And they write all kinds of things like "My Son's not feeling well and please visit and I'm sure he'll get all right if you just come across and see us." And they invite me across for their weddings and I don't even know who they are.'

Dipika Chikhlia was also approached by officials from the BJP party and asked to stand for Parliament. At that time she knew nothing of politics. She agreed to stand for a semi-rural constituency in Baroda, some hundred miles north of Bombay. She maintains that she made it clear to the electorate that she had decided she was a serious candidate, not just an actress whose only qualification for Parliament was that she had played a mythological figure in a Hindu soap opera. How important was it to the electorate that she had played Sita? 'I think Sita played a little part initially,' she says, 'but then I took it over and I made sure that was only one of the things' which resulted in her vote. Her opponents disagree. Mrinal Gore, a representative of the Janapadall party and an experienced politician, is in no doubt as to the significance of the role Dipika played. 'Sita is adored by Indian women. So naturally she caught the most advantage of that. How was Dipika selected to be a candidate? I don't know. She had nothing to do with politics.' Ms Gore believes that in rural areas there was clear confusion between the actress and the role she played. 'They thought she was the real Sita,' says Ms Gore. 'They thought she represents the values they had in adoring Sita.'

We travelled out into the rural areas of Dipika's constituency to see if this could be true – if the propaganda power of entertainment television was such that some people actually believed they had voted for a mythological character. It would be more remarkable than if J.R. Ewing himself had been elected to office. After all, J.R. was supposed to be a character in the real world, a Texas oilman, and real Texas oilmen exist. But Sita was a goddess. The reality was put best by Avi Sabavalla, a local businesswoman. 'Let me make it clear that people are perfectly aware out here that it's not the real Sita. But all the same they felt that since this person had played the role of Sita, it was right and proper to give her the vote and maybe if they didn't give her the vote it would invite some serious consequences – evil consequences. It's a superstition. You see, on one hand they're aware that this is a human who has taken the role of Sita, but on the other hand they also feel that if they did not give her the vote they might be doing some sin.'

Ramanand Sagar is unequivocal about the reason why Dipika was elected. 'Five hundred, two thousand ladies came out with their lamps here in Baroda and did their worship to her because for them it was Sita. They were voting for Sita because they saw Sita in her.' As a result of such TV-inspired devotion Dipika is now the Honourable Member for the Baroda district, responsible for 1.6 million constituents.

The chairman of the local BJP denies either that his party made capital out of the series or that Dipika was elected because of the part she played. Such views are hard to countenance given that in both cases it was the BJP who approached the actors and not the other way around. But one can understand why the BJP has to maintain that TV was not a factor. If they accepted that the party approached an actress solely on the basis of the part she played in a mythological soap opera then doubts might be cast on her legitimacy as a candidate to represent more than a million constituents. Mrinal Gore of the Janapadall has no such inhibitions about commenting on the fact that this seems a strange way to select and elect an MP. 'It is not only strange,' she told me. 'It is absurd for democracy if such people are elected just because they have played the part of Sita. It is really absurd.'

Perhaps some people would say: 'This was India, these people were semi-literate. Television entertainment may have meant she could be elected, but such a phenomenon couldn't work elsewhere.' But it already has.

The power of the chat show host

Silvio Santos not only owns his own TV network in Brazil, but also presents an enormously successful game show every Sunday. The show is pure entertainment. A panel of guests is asked to judge a variety of different acts – a transvestite singer, a dwarf juggler, that sort of thing. Through it all Mr Santos prances with a merry quip on his lips; he is the Brazilian Bob Monkhouse. At the time of the last Brazilian Presidential election Mr Santos decided, rather late in the day, that he would stand for office on an effective policy of 'no policies' – his theme best paraphrased as: 'You've seen me on TV so you know you can trust me.' He immediately went to the top of the polls before having to withdraw because of a technicality – his election nomination papers had not been returned before the necessary deadline. If it hadn't been for this, he might actually have become President of Brazil. Ironically, it was rumoured that the only reason Mr Santos's network had been granted its franchise to broadcast in the first place was because state officials believed that as an entertainment network it presented no political threat.

Carlos Palenquez is a Bolivian who started his career as a pop singer. He went on to own his own TV station in La Paz, the capital. In the mid-eighties he started hosting a programme called *Open Tribunal of the People*, in which ordinary people rang in and asked for advice and help. In 1988 he launched his own political party, called Conscience of the Fatherland, and the following year was fourth in the Presidential elections out of a field of ten. In 1989 he narrowly failed to become Mayor of La Paz; now he's concentrating on running for President in 1993. Mr Palenquez is taken seriously as a politician because he hosts a television programme.

Ricardo Belmont was a Peruvian disc jockey who used to appear on a show called *The Sky's the Limit*, but his popularity really began to take off when he started to host charity telethon appeals. He created his own political party called the Civic Works Movement and entered the November 1989 mayoral elections in Lima. He shunned campaign rallies, promoting his candidacy almost exclusively through his own television station. He won, beating seven experienced politicians despite the fact that he had no real credible political experience.

So here are three examples of TV stars who have entered politics – entered it, moreover, with a substantial amount of linkage between their screen persona and their political persona. It is not hard to see how a destitute Brazilian might believe that a game show host whom he has watched every week and come to trust might be the person to help him with his real problems. Or how a Peruvian peasant might think that the man to put things right is that nice man who runs the charity telethon. Or a starving Bolivian that the man he and his family can rely on is the kind presenter of the television advice programme.

Is this so very different from the phenomenon of electing a

mythological character to Parliament? For television presenters are to some extent mythological characters, carefully protected by their production teams. One of the biggest shocks I ever received in television was on my induction course at the BBC, when a famous presenter came to give the trainees a talk. As he walked in it was as if I was seeing an old friend, a kindly uncle with whom I had grown up, a man I could trust. He stood at the podium and his gentle face broke into a snarl. 'Who bloody arranged the parking, eh?' he demanded menacingly. The image of him I had gained from TV was shattered.

Some might argue that the fact that our idols have feet of clay is nothing new – political consultants tell similar stories about the politicians in their charge. But there is something new and different about TV presenters. Because of their profession they are cosseted and protected from situations which the ordinary politician has to face head-on; protected in ways that Michael Deaver could only in his wildest dreams have used to protect Reagan. A TV presenter is always operating at a level above that of normal political accountability. It can be – indeed is – perfectly possible that a TV presenter can project an image, week in week out, which is totally alien from his or her real personality. The programme's production team will know the truth, but it will be hidden from everyone else – especially from journalists.

Nor is there a guarantee that the TV personality's secrets will be revealed by the election process. For it is clear from the South American experience that the TV presenter candidate will rarely be held to account during the election itself. The very reason he is standing is his awareness of the power and strength of the medium, and therefore that his campaign should be conducted through television rather than other more conventional political campaigning techniques – techniques which traditionally lead to accountability.

There is no reason why this could not happen in the West. In Italy the porn star La Cicciolina was made an MP in 1989, partly as a result of the popularity she had generated through her chat show appearances. No one could have been in any doubt as to the extent of her political gifts, yet she was elected to Parliament. The celebrity chairman of the real Madrid football club, Roberto Gil, is also Mayor of Marbella. (After becoming Mayor, he began presenting a titillating light entertainment programme called 'Gil Y Gil' which is recorded in Marbella.) In Britain David Icke, a man who used to be a sports reporter on BBC2, received extensive coverage when he made a series of less than totally rational announcements about the forthcoming end of the world.

The question the propagandist should ask is this. Would La Cicciolina be an MP, would Roberto Gil be Mayor of Marbella and would David Icke have received the publicity he did without previous celebrity? If the answer is no, as it surely must be, then it is clear that the TV presenter has considerable latent political power which can be exploited. After all, the TV presenter is the one person who has clearly learnt how to look and act on television, and who has already had experience both of fame and of developing a screen persona which is ideally suited to the demands of the medium.

The fact that being a TV presenter in no material way fits you for effective political office is hardly relevant. Throughout time the political propagandist has only dealt with hard reality. In today's television-dominated world only an idealist would demand politicians who are actually qualified to govern.

Notes

1. Nugent, Nicholas: *Rajiv Gandhi – Son of a Dynasty*

Conclusion

At the end, what are we left with? Certainly with a world in which television has fundamentally altered political discourse – with the United States the clearest example of a democratic nation held in thrall to the medium. But should we care? And if we do care, what should we do about it?

As discussed in Chapter 1, since television works best as a medium of entertainment then it follows that political propaganda works best when it is based on entertainment criteria. In the USA the logical consequences are that the fitness for office of political leaders is examined and defined in entertainment terms. American leaders must have a sense of humour; they must be pragmatic enough to respond quickly to the pollsters' instructions; and above all they must be likeable. It follows that since television dictates that we make a decision about an *individual* then the voter can no longer rely on party policy – he can no longer vote for a candidate because he likes the policy but dislikes the man. Consultants like Joe Slade-White see this as a step forward in the democratic process. He believes that television 'can make a candidate who is unknown instantly known and I think that to some extent it has broken the hold that parties have on the process. It has rewritten the rules and it's accelerated change.' Raymond Strother is another consultant who does not recall the days of party loyalty in the USA with particular affection. 'Remember how it was before?' he says. 'When you had a strong party organization you had ward leaders and the ward leader would knock on the door and say, "Miss Smith, I would like for you to vote for our man Mr Doe. Mr Doe is one of us. . . . Yes, he's one of us." And he leaves. Now does she know anything? All she knows is he's endorsed by the party fathers who have put the stamp of approval on this candidate and that's all this woman knows. Is that worse than television? I think that's pretty trivial too.'

Strother makes his point persuasively, but he misses one key advantage of the party system – if you vote along party lines you know the policies you are supporting. The Reaganesque situation of voting into office a man because you like him but dislike his policies cannot occur. And it is much easier to call a politician to account for a failure to deliver on policy than for a failure to deliver on personality. As Professor Postman puts it, 'The politics I grew up with and certainly my father and mother grew up with was a politics of party, in that you tended to vote for a party because that party represented in some clear way your sociological class and your economic interest. Therefore, politics was rational and it didn't make a difference in a sense who was the party candidate.'

When Postman, who comes from a family of diehard Democrats, was a young man and about to vote for the first time he decided that the Democratic candidate on offer was something of a fool and he preferred the Republican candidate. He mentioned his proposed choice to his father, who responded: 'Are you crazy? Do you want the Republicans in power?' Postman replied: 'But the Democrat is a fool and he's corrupt.' To which his father answered: 'Well, Democrat candidates are all fools and most of them are corrupt, but the important thing is the party is in because they represent the working class.' Postman told me he believes that 'There is something rational about that'. Once candidates are voted in on individual terms – essentially on criteria of 'likeability' – rather than on the basis of whether the policies they propose are in the voters' self-interest, then we do indeed have a new kind of politics, one in which rationality is not essential.

The sheer cost of American propaganda campaigns is another way in which television has caused a fundamental change in the democratic process. Money is an all-important campaign prerequisite. Without it you cannot be elected to public office because you cannot be elected without television, and television must be purchased. This simple fact has enormous repercussions. For the people with the money are not, generally speaking, about to give their hard-earned cash away out of charity. They want something in return, and often that something results in special interest group pressure on candidates as described by Frank Greer in Chapter 2. There is another insidious consequence, too. The money men are not unlike crude Hollywood producers, who never put money into a prospective film idea which has an untried or potentially uncommercial formula. There is precious little idealism in Hollywood, and precious little idealism amongst the money men who finance campaigns. But imagine a situation in which a cross-section of interested and informed voters, rather than a group of money men, are choosing the candidate. The voters might well be influenced by the idealism or charisma of a black man or a woman, so much so that they would choose him over another, more obviously 'electable', candidate. It's hard to see how hardened money men would take such a risk. Money is a notoriously inhibiting commodity, especially in politics where the betting must always, other things being equal, be on the incumbent in today's TV-dominated world.

There is also evidence that the grind of daily fund-raising causes talented candidates to leave politics. Governor Reubin Askew of Florida gave up his Senate race in mid-campaign in 1988 because he could not abide the harassment of constant fund-raising.[1] Candidates inevitably spend less time in contact with ordinary voters and more time on the phone pleading for campaign contributions. Hubert Humphrey was heard to remark, after leaving a hotel room where he had spent hours on the phone trying to raise money for his 1972 bid for President, that: 'It's making us all beggars. I hate it worse than anything else I have to do.'[2]

Indeed, is today's TV propaganda simply turning the electorate off politics to the extent that they no longer bother to vote? In the 1988 US Presidential election only 50.16 per cent of those eligible bothered to vote at all. Can this be laid at the door of the propagandists who created a notoriously mean and spiteful campaign? Senator John Danforth believes it can. Speaking in the Senate in 1990, he said, 'Political campaigns turn the stomach of the average voter. Most people, by the time election day occurs, are sick of the whole process. I don't know what academics have concluded, but I know what I have concluded just on the basis of talking to my own constituents. They are sick about modern politics and they are particularly sick about what they see on television.'

Not surprisingly, many of the political consultants disagree with this analysis. They categorically deny responsibility for the low voter turnout in 1988. The most vociferous defender of the consultant's art is one of those most often attacked, Greg Stevens. 'That's baloney,' he says of Senator Danforth's criticisms. 'This country and your country have been engaging in what is now labelled as negative campaigning since the beginning of time. If you cannot criticize your opponent's record there's no point in running.' Stevens is adamant that 'no one has been able to prove that there is a correlation between so called negative campaigning or negative advertising and the decrease in voter turn out.' Instead, the cause of the problem is 'a frustration on the part of the voters about what is happening once these people get elected.' Some might feel Stevens's argument is reminiscent of the objections the tobacco companies made to the initially tentative findings that there might be a link between smoking and cancer. Certainly, in this case there remains a reasonable hypothesis that the quality of campaigning is resulting in cynicism amongst the voters.

There is another way, however, in which the emphasis of the campaign on the quality of the individual rather than the policies of the party endangers the democratic system. In the words of Raymond Strother: 'In certain circumstances you can elect real dummies.' Because of the lack of emphasis on any examination and testing of policy, and the consequent concentration on personality, even some consultants like Strother believe that 'strange, kookie, people' can be elected. It may be that such politicians serve only one term before they are found out, or it may be that once in office they acquire propagandists who can protect them, but even if they only serve one term they can do enormous damage. Of course, 'strange, kookie' people could be elected under the party system, but at least (and it bears repeating), under the party system, the issues and policies they were elected on ensure greater accountability.

Part of the problem is that the very people who rely most on television to form their political views tend to be the least politically sophisticated in society. Almost by definition they are the ones who read neither the quality papers nor political books. It's hardly surprising, then, that these are people who can be persuaded to elect previously unqualified chat show hosts or actresses. But it's hard to blame the voters in such circumstances, and harder to blame the politicians who use television in such a way. All the politicians are doing is exploiting the particular strengths of the medium. Who could have predicted that television, left unrestrained, would eventually turn politics into a world in which a chat show host enters a political race at a considerable advantage over, say, a university professor or even another politician? Well, Goebbels could. But even he believed in the necessity of censorship as well as entertainment – censorship which is, as Postman says, 'the tribute tyrants pay to the assumption that a public knows the difference between serious discourse and entertainment – and cares'. Yet censorship in countries which provide entertainment on television hardly seems necessary. The only censorship required is the censorship that operates in each viewer's mind as he or she turns away from the news and on to the soap. One need look no further than newly democratic Brazil to see the consequences of such logic. In this country which suffers appalling privation, where millions sleep and die on the streets, where millions more live in unsanitary shacks called *favelas*, almost all that can be seen on TV is either sport or soap operas, known as *novelas*.

On one occasion I was filming an entire family in one *favela*, inaccurately called Hill of Pleasures, high above Rio. In the middle of telling us of their desperate plight they stopped, turned round and sat down close to their TV – the only electrical appliance in the shack – to catch the latest *novela* from TV Globo. Like the majority of *novelas*, this one featured the glamorous lives of the rich and famous – the limos, the yachts, the parties – and the poor family sat entranced. It was salutary that they made no clamour for electoral reform, they voiced no objection that they were unable to watch investigative current affairs programmes. There was no need of censorship to control these people. Such was their craving for release from the squalor of their workaday lives that TV soap operas had become as essential to their survival as the very air they breathed.

It was Julius Caesar who remarked that he had 'no need of the army to control the people of Rome' because he had discovered that his fellow citizens could be diverted by the bloody 'entertainment' spectacles he provided at the Roman Circus. A modern Caesar might well speak of the soap opera in the same way.

If the worth of a TV programme is judged solely on the number of people who watch it, and how much it costs to make, then it is to be expected that the mass audience channels will concentrate on entertainment. Examples all round the world show that detailed political coverage on television is a minority interest. The success of CNN illustrates primarily not that there is a market for information on television, but that to compete with entertainment news must be snappier and more ephemeral. Attention span is all. Their *Hollywood Minute* of film star news delivered slickly in sixty seconds encapsulates this formula. In any event, CNN will only ever broadcast to a minority of homes. The majority want a TV service consisting only of action drama, comedy, chat and game shows – the four great pillars of entertainment-based output. There will still be some news on the main network channels, but despite the best efforts of people like Dottie Lynch there is no reason to suppose that the balance in news coverage will turn from entertainment to education. News programmes in America may still get high ratings, but as one network accountant put it to me: 'They're just not cost-effective. We could deliver the same ratings for less money if we replaced the news with a game show.'

The main effort of the American TV propagandist is directed at the political commercial, and the freedom of political consultants to say what they like in these ads is seen in some quarters as simply an exercise of their rights under the American Constitution, where free speech is guaranteed to all. But it is a curious form of free speech that is granted only to those who have enough money to exercise it. There is little reason to suppose that the form of these ads will change without external pressure – they are too effective for that. It is true that some evolution in their content can be detected from the crude biographical ads, through the emotive 'Wallop Ride' type ads, via the nasty negatives, now to the funny negatives. But it is a grave mistake to assume that the apparently gentler ads in any way represent a move forward. Joe Slade-White's 'Bodyguard' ad is a beautiful piece of television and a misleading piece of information. Tony Schwartz's laughing ad aimed at Spiro Agnew is very funny, but it does not help democratic discourse.

If the fundamental structure and grammar of the ads are more or less set, what will change is the 'delivery system'. Consultants spend almost as much time placing their ads in the right catchment area as they do making them. As polling becomes more and more sophisticated it will be possible to make a variety of ads around one specific theme and to direct those ads not just geographically into each different area of a constituency, but to use cable, and the audience profile of the average cable viewer, to appeal to particular socio-economic groups. It may even be possible to direct ads individually at the voter. Robert Squier, veteran Democratic consultant, painted this vision of the future:

> At the beginning of the evening you would get a short, simple quiz on your interactive cable system. You would be offered an opportunity to see a free movie if you'd answer a few sports questions, a few political questions, some other question, a lot of political questions. We wouldn't have to ask a lot of demographic questions, because if you were a cable subscriber for more than a year, we would have all we needed to know about you from other quizzes. We would know how much you vote, how you vote, what kind of programmes you watch, how many times you switch over to the X-rated channel. Then you'd take the test. The system would determine your particular brand of undecidedness, based on previous polling in the population. The computer would then select the particular tape it needed to persuade you. It would have been pre-tested in focus groups. Then it would play on your TV that night, on everything you'd watch on cable. Later in the evening you'd be given another test, asking some of the same questions. If we've persuaded you, we'd know it right then.[3]

Squier's vision is designed to talk up the glories of his profession. Consultants are a long way away from having not so much the technical sophistication to fulfil Squier's idea as the money – the problem with such targeting is that it would be fearsomely expensive. But it is possible. And if propagandists go this route it will simply mean that more money, not less, will be needed for a campaign. It is, of course, in the interest of the consultants that campaigning gets more expensive. As well as a fee, most consultants charge a percentage of the 'media spend' – the more the ads cost to show, the more they earn.

At the heart of the issue of the consultants' work there is, or should be, a debate about the power of television to act as a propaganda tool. That debate is lacking in America. Mark Fowler, who in 1981 was Reagan's nominee for Chairman of the Federal Communications Commission, put the non-interventionist case best when he said of television that it was 'just another appliance – it's a toaster with pictures'.

If such attitudes prevail, there is a real danger that Robert Spero's prophetic words might be realized: 'Someday someone is going to sneak into elective office behind a shield of these hit and run commercials who will make Watergate look like child's play. For all anybody knows, that person is already in office – somewhere.'[4]

So what should be done? This is a case where Americans can learn from the British. The British electorate are protected from most of the abuses inherent in the American system by two things, money and time. If airtime was guaranteed free to each party in America, the system would immediately improve. The variety and quality of people who could then put themselves forward as candidates would improve enormously. No longer would it be a disqualification if you were in every way an excellent candidate but were simply poor and did not have rich friends. Both blacks and women, currently under-represented in politics, could come forward in greater numbers. Because the airtime would be allocated chiefly to the major parties this would also increase the power of the party; this would, in turn, mean that candidates would stand on a party ticket of policies in a more definite way than they do at present. But this would not mean that the major parties could return to the era of the 'smoke-filled room'. The qualifications of free airtime at the primary stage of the electoral process could be independent of party approval.

The candidates would still have to pay to make their own ads. But ads can be both cheap and effective, for it is not the cost of the ads themselves that makes campaigns expensive, but the fact that it is expensive to show them. Free airtime would be split equally between the major parties, which would get rid of the ludicrous situation in which a candidate can at the minute simply 'outshout' his opponent by paying to have his ads shown again and again. A provision could be made so that anyone could stand for office outside of the party structure, but that they would have to pay for their airtime – this would further prevent the major parties exercising dominance.

Allied to abolishing the cost of showing political ads should be a commitment to make the minimum length of each commercial five minutes. The British experience is that it is seldom possible to run emotion-driven, issue-free content for more than a minute or so. Consultants would no doubt try to find ways round this restriction, perhaps by splitting the five minutes into ten commercials; but it could well be that ten similar political commercials watched one after the other have a numbing effect. It would be worth a try.

Unfortunately it is hard to see how any of these proposals have much of a chance of success. The problem is that it will take a large number of elected officials to execute change; yet these very officials have been almost to a man placed in office by the techniques which they would be trying to change. The potential for charges of 'hypocrisy' is enormous. In addition there is a substantial number of politicians, academics and consultants who think that the American democratic system is the finest in the world, and that any attempt to change it and legislate particular aspects of it is the equivalent of a proposal to burn the American flag.

But just because there is little hope of changing the system wholeheartedly does not mean that the issue should not be discussed. For it may be that useful, immediate and practical changes can be affected around the edges of the problem. One welcome development is the use of 'ad-watch' columns in newspapers, where space is devoted to analysing the truth or untruth of particular campaign adverts. The only difficulty with this device is that if more people were reading the sort of papers that carried 'ad-watch' in the first place there would be less distortion. The fact is that most people don't get their campaign news from the papers, they get it from television; which is why the role and responsibility of the electronic news media are enormous. They can't hide behind the Donaldson doctrine that the White House correspondent is not there to 'set an agenda'; they must be proactive in the way that Dottie Lynch of CBS espouses. But again there are problems: not just that it is a somewhat romantic notion that the networks will set out to lead opinion, given that it is the politicians who ultimately decide their fate, but probably also because in order to criticize an ad it is necessary to show it, and by showing it you give the work more exposure. Remember how Deaver demonstrated that on TV the picture is mightier than the word.

One of the greatest ironies of current political propaganda is that the master of the visual is one of the champions of reform. 'I am not happy with television coverage of either politics or government,' Deaver told me. 'I simply adjusted to what the television moguls had decided was gonna sell. I didn't say, "We're gonna put Ronald Reagan up for sixty seconds." He was speaking for twenty minutes. They took sixty seconds out of it for the evening news.' Deaver believes that the networks let the public (and by implication the President's propagandists) dictate too easily the length of coverage of important national issues. 'The networks, if they wanted to in this country, could stand up and say, "We're not gonna cover you guys any more unless you give us an hour – a one-hour-long interview." I mean what would we do? We'd have to say, "Yes".' Not necessarily, given that there are three rival terrestrial networks plus CNN, and Deaver himself was adept at playing them off against each other. Still, Deaver is genuine in his belief that 'It's really lousy the job we do in this country in informing the public where our candidate stands on the issues. The closest we get to it, and I still think this isn't well run, are these debates.' Deaver's view is that America should borrow something akin to Prime Minister's Question Time from the British system and 'Put both parties – the two nominees – of the major parties in this country in the well of the House of Representatives and for two hours let the Congress ask them any questions they want to. Not the media. Now one of the ways we judge our candidates for President is how well they do on their feet. How well they deal with a political situation. How well they're gonna get along with these legislators. Wouldn't that be a better way to do it?'

It's ironical that the man who controlled access to Reagan so brilliantly during the 1984 election should now be advocating open debate, but he was not the only professional 'communicator' I met who expressed a wide-eyed fascination with the exchanges they had seen televised from the British parliament. They thought it remarkable that members of the British Cabinet were subjected to Opposition questions which often turned into ill-concealed excuses for abuse. But one aspect of the British parliamentary process drew derision from the Americans – the party political broadcasts. 'If I did your political broadcasts I'd be out of business next season,' says Raymond Strother. 'They're too dull. They wouldn't hold the attention of the American audience. But remember you're still the country that runs snooker matches on the television.'

America has much to learn from Britain in the restriction of the power of the TV propagandists. But the learning process has so far been all one way – from America to Britain. However, none of this means that the British can be complacent. There were several propaganda techniques used during the 1992 campaign which revealed American influence. Both the Labour party's election broadcast featuring a small child waiting for an ear operation, and the Conservatives' biographical portrait of John Major were light years away from the traditional information-driven heritage of British election broadcasts.

The British did escape the attentions of Roger Ailes. I understand that prior to the election there was a secret meeting in New York between him and Shaun Woodward. After some discussion Woodward apparently decided not to progress contacts between the Conservatives and the Media Team. For students of propaganda this was a pity. A Tory election campaign masterminded by Roger Ailes would have been revealing.

The Conservative campaign was similar to many American ones in that it was driven by personalities and not issues. When called upon to think of positive reasons why anyone should vote Tory the local party supporter who knocked on my door was quick to retort: 'Vote for John Major,' he said, 'You don't want Kinnock in, do you?' And this was the pattern repeated over the country. The campaign sought not so much a vote for the Conservatives, but a vote for John Major. Could this be a drift away from the idea of voting for a party, the concept so valued by American academics like Professor Postman and seemingly lost to the United States? One way of testing this hypothesis is by examining the uniformity of the swing of the vote away from one party and towards another, a swing which on election night varied widely from seat to seat. It seems clear that voters were influenced not just by their opinion of John Major or Neil Kinnock or Paddy Ashdown, but by their opinion of their own individual MP. Some MPs who should have lost on the predicted nationwide swing actually won, leaving one American consultant I talked to after the election unequivocally to conclude: 'That's personality politics you're seeing.'

Another key fact the student of communication should notice about the last election was how it was yet again the ordinary voter, not the highly paid interviewers, who unsettled the politicians. *Election Call*, in which each day one leading political figure was subjected to phone-in questions from ordinary voters, was compulsive viewing. Poor Tony Blair from Labour's front bench team was floored by persistent questions from a woman who felt her business would be affected by Labour's planned minimum wage, and Michael Heseltine was called to account for his actions in standing against Mrs Thatcher. *Election Call* is one programme no American political consultant would let his candidate near.

In communication terms the view persists, as the editorial in the *People* newspaper put it, that, 'In 1987, Labour won the campaign but lost the election. Now it has happened again. An efficient and clever campaign. A disappointing defeat.'

Watching the glitz of the Labour rallies it's easy to see how this myth has occurred, but myth it must remain. The first opinion poll published at the start of the campaign showed Labour on 41 per cent and the Conservatives on 38 per cent. The General Election revealed the Conservatives on 41.9 per cent and Labour on 34.4 per cent. Even allowing for a 3 per cent margin of error in the initial poll this demonstrates an extraordinary turn around by the Conservatives during the course of the election campaign. So how can the Conservatives be said to have lost the campaign? Dave Hill, Labour's Director of Communication, primarily blamed the Tory dominated tabloids for their defeat, but the press has always been Tory dominated and still Labour governments have been elected. The truth is that despite its slickness the Labour campaign never managed to answer the Tory questions about their tax policy.

Neil Kinnock made at least one textbook communication mistake during the last week of the campaign. He refused to say where he stood on the issue of proportional representation. Instead he maintained that whilst he had his own personal view he would not be telling anyone what it was until after a committee of inquiry had submitted their report. It's not hard to see how Neil Kinnock's words would have made him appear devious – not that it is necessarily the case that the politician has to always let the voter know where he stands on every issue in order to ensure success. A classic example of this was Richard Nixon who was able to appear firm and decisive whilst not committing himself, often using the form of words, 'Let me make one thing absolutely clear, we are going to look carefully at this issue before coming to a decision.' But simply to imply, as Neil Kinnock appeared to, 'I've got my own view but I'm not going to tell you what it is,' invites distrust.

Analysis conducted by Channel 4 news during the campaign demonstrated that a panel of representative voters consistently said they disliked the Conservative election broadcasts more than those of the other parties, particularly a Tory film which showed (with the graphic use of balls and chains) how Labour's economic policies would spell disaster for the country. But as any American political consultant knows, a focus group almost never admits to approving of a negative ad. Viewers always claim to enjoy positive upbeat messages more. Yet when it comes to actual voting it is the negative ads that work. In the privacy of the voting booth the negative message that has been planted in the voter's mind is often a deciding factor in the outcome of the election.

As the 1992 election demonstrated, British political campaigns are becoming more American in style. But the safeguards of ten-minute election broadcasts, free political air-time, vigilant journalists, and politicians prepared to answer detailed questions about their proposals, mean that there is some way to go before we need fear the election of a Dan Quayle to one of the great offices of State. Even a giant of his profession like Michael Deaver would find it hard to scrabble a living on this side of the Atlantic. Whether this state of affairs is his loss but our gain is for the voter to decide.

Notes

1. Germond, Jack, and Jules Witcover: *Whose Broad Stripes and Bright Stars?*

2. Ibid

3. Diamond, Edwin, and Stephen Bates: *The Spot – The Rise of Political Advertising on Television*

4. Spero, Robert: *The Duping of the American Voter*

Bibliography

Adatto, Kiku: *Sound Bite Democracy: Network Evening News Presidential Campaign Coverage 1968 and 1988* (Barone Center for Press, Politics and Public Policy, John F. Kennedy School of Government, Harvard University, 1990).

Ailes, Roger: *You Are the Message* (Doubleday, New York, 1988)

Brewer,Derek S.: *Symbolic Stories* (D. S. Brewer/Rowman and Littlefield, Cambridge, 1980)

Broder, David S.: *Behind the Front Page – A Candid Look at How the News is Made* (Simon and Schuster, New York 1988).

Cannon, Lou: *President Reagan – The Role of a Lifetime* (Simon and Schuster, New York 1991)

Cantril, Albert H.: *The Opinion Connection – Polling, Politis, and the Press* (Congressional Quarterly Inc., Washington DC, 1991)

Chagall, David: *The New Kingmakers* (Harcourt Brace Jovanovich, New York 1981).

Clark, Eric: *The Want Makers* (Hodder and Stoughton, London, 1988)

Cockerell, Michael: *Live from Number 10* (Faber and Faber, London, 1988)

Cook, Mark, and Robert McHenry: *Sexual Attraction* (Pergamon Press, Oxford, 1978)

Deaver, Michael K., with Micky Herskowitz: *Behind the Scenes* (William Morrow, New York, 1987)

Diamond, Edwin, and Stephen Bates: *The Spot – The Rise of Political Advertising on Television* (MIT Press, Cambridge, Massachusettts,. 1984)

Ehrlichman, John: *Witnessed Power* (Simon and Schuster, New York, 1982)

Fallon, Ivan: *The Brothers – The Rise and Rise of Saatchi and Saatchi* (Hutchinson, London, 1988)

Fox, Stephen: *The Mirror Makers* (Random House, New York, 1984)

Germond, Jack, and Jules Witcover: *Whose Broad Stripes and Bright Stars?* (Warner Books Inc., New York, 1989)

Goebbels, J.: *The Goebbels Diaries*, translated and edited by Louis P.Lockner (Hamish Hamilton, London, 1948)

Goebbels, J.: *The Goebbels Diaries – The Last Days*, edited and introduced by Hugh Trevor-Roper (Secker and Warburg, London, 1978)

Goebbles, J.: *Die Tagebücer von Josepb Goebbels*, 4 vols (K.G. Saur Verlag, Munich, 1987)

Goebbels, J.: *My Part in Germany's Fight*, translated by Dr Kurt Fiedler (London, 1935)

Govender, Robert: *Nicolae Ceausescu and the Romanian Road to Socialism* (Unified Printers and Publishers, London, 1982)

Grabber, Doris A.: *Mass Media and American Politics* (Congressional Quarterly Inc., Washington DC, 1989)

Graham, Fred: *Happy Talk* (Random House, New York, 1990)

Greenfield, Jeff: *The Real Campaign* (Summit Books, New York, 1982)

Halberstam, David: *The Powers That Be* (Alfred A. Knopf, New York, 1979)

Haldeman, H.R.: *The Ends of Power* (New York Times Books, New York, 1978)

Heiber, Helmut: *Goebbels* (Hawthorn Books Inc., London, 1972)

Hertsgaard, Mark: *On Bended Knee – The Press and the Reagan Presidency* (Schocken Books, New York, 1989)

Hippler, Fritz: *Die Verstrickung* (Mehr Wissen, Düsseldorf, 1989)

Hughes, Colin, and Patrick Wintour: *Labour Rebuilt* (4th Estate, London, 1990)

Jamieson, Kathleen Hall: *Packaging the Presidency* (Oxford University Press, New York, 1984)

Kern, Montague: *Thirty-Second Politics: Political Advertising in the eighties* (Praeger Publishers, New York, 1989)

Kershaw, Ian: *The Hitler Myth – Image and Reality in the Third Reich* (Oxford University Press 1987)

King, Martin Luther Jnr: *A Testament of Hope* (HarperCollins New York, 1991)

McGinniss, Joe: *The Selling of the President, 1968* (Trident, New York, 1969)

McLuhan, Marshall: *Understanding Media* (McGraw Hill, New York, 1964)

Matthews, Christopher: *Hardball – How Politics is Played – Told By One Who Knows the Game* (Summit Books, New York, 1988)

Meissner. Hans Otto: *Magda Goebbels – The First Lady of the Third Reich* (Sidgwick and Jackson, London, 1980)

Nimmo, Dan: *The Political Persuaders* (Prentice-Hall, New Jersey, 1970)

Noonan, Peggy: *What I Saw at the Revolution* (Random House, New York, 1987)

Nugent, Nicholas: *Rajiv Gandhi – Son of a Dynasty* (BBC Books, London, 1990)

Paletz, David L., and Robert M. Intman: *Media Power Politics* (Macmillan, New York, 1981)

Popkin, Samuel L.: *The Reasoning Voter* (Chicago University Press, 1991)

Postman, Neil: *Amusing Ourselves to Death* (Viking Penguin, New York, 1985)

Powell, Jody: *The Other Side of the Story* (William Morrow, New York, 1984)

Ranney, Austin: *Channels of Power, the Impact of TV on American Politids* (American Enterprise Institute for Public Policy Research, Washington DC, 1983)

Sabato, Larry J.: *The Rise of Political Consultants* (Basic Books, New York 1981)

Schwartz, Tony: *Media – the Second God* (Random House, New York, 1981)

Shea, Michael: *Influence – How to Make the System Work for You* (Century Hutchinson, London, 1988)

Spero, Robert: *The Duping of the American Voter* (Lippincott and Crowell, Philadelphia PA, 1980)

Suetonius: *The Twelve Caesars*, translated by Robert Graves (Penguin, London 1979)

Taylor, Paul: *See How They Run – Electing the President in an Age of Mediaocracy* (Alfred A. Knopf, New York, 1990)

Von Oven, Wilfred: *Mit Goebbels bis zum Ende* (Buenos Aires, 1949)

Welch, David, ed.: *Nazi Propaganda* (Croom Helm Ltd, Beckenham, 1983)

Welch, David: *Propaganda and the German Cinema 1933–45* (Oxford University Press, 1983)

White, Theodore H.: *The Making of the President 1972* (Jonathan Cape, London, 1973)

Witcover, Jules: *Marathon – The Pursuit of the Presidency, 1972–1976* (Viking Press, New York, 1977)

Index